Aardman presents
Wallace & Gromit™

The Bootiful Game

Titan Books

Wallace & Gromit™
The Bootiful Game

HB ISBN 1 84023 943 3
PB ISBN 1 84023 948 4

Published by Titan Books,
a division of Titan Publishing Group Ltd.
144 Southwark Street
London SE1 0UP
In association with Aardman Animation Ltd.

Grateful thanks and salutations to Dick Hansom and Rachael Carpenter
at Aardman Animations, and David Barraclough, Jamie Boardman,
Bob Kelly, Angie Thomas and Katy Wild at Titan Books.

A CIP catalogue record for this title is available at the British Library.

Hardback edition: May 2005
Paperback edition: September 2005

1 3 5 7 9 10 8 6 4 2

Printed in Italy.

What did you think of this book? We love to
hear from our readers. Please email us at:
readerfeedback@titanemail.com, or write to us
at the above address.

www.titanbooks.com

Aardman presents

Wallace & Gromit™

The Bootiful Game

Original story by Simon Furman and Ian Rimmer

Written by Ian Rimmer

Drawn by Brian Williamson

Inked by Bambos Georgiou

Coloured by Kev Hopgood

Lettered by Richard Starkings

Designed by Caroline Grimshaw

Edited by Simon Furman & Nick Jones

Wallace and Gromit created by Nick Park

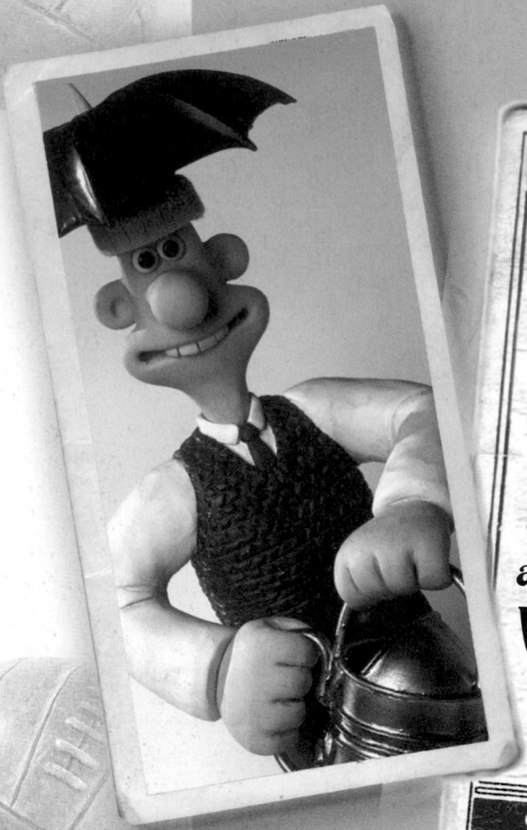

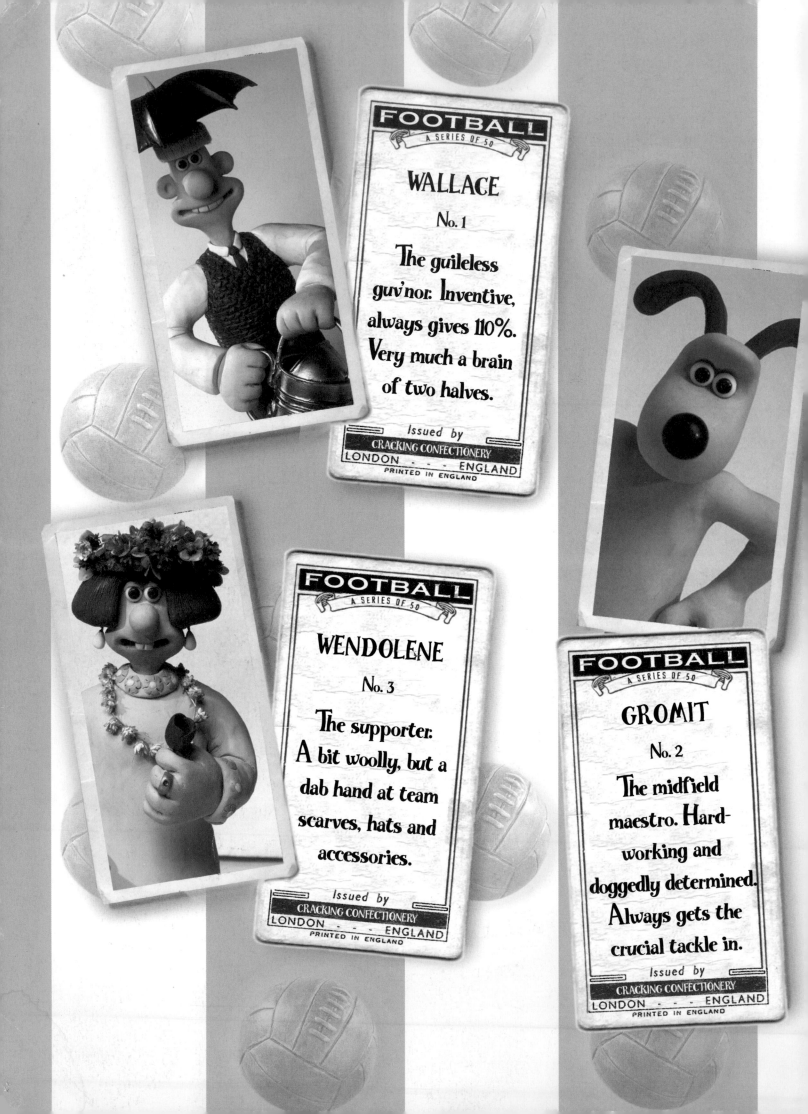

FOOTBALL

A SERIES OF 50

WALLACE

No. 1

The guileless guv'nor: Inventive, always gives 110%. Very much a brain of two halves.

Issued by
CRACKING CONFECTIONERY
LONDON - - - ENGLAND
PRINTED IN ENGLAND

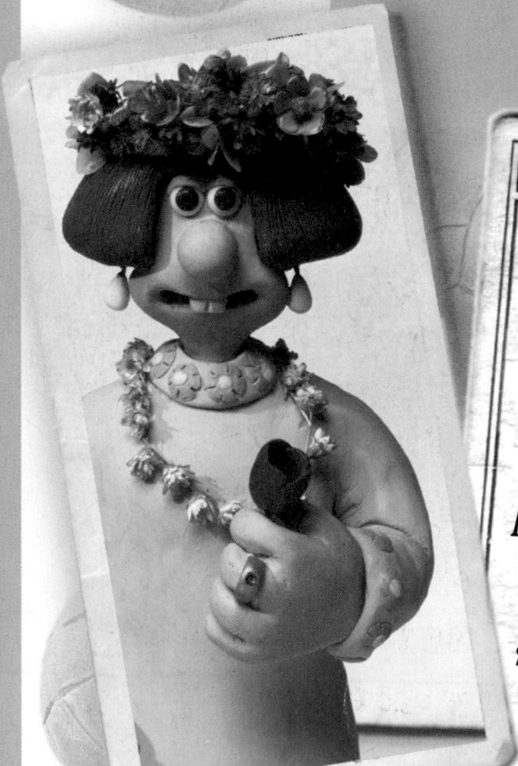

FOOTBALL

A SERIES OF 50

WENDOLENE

No. 3

The supporter: A bit woolly, but a dab hand at team scarves, hats and accessories.

Issued by
CRACKING CONFECTIONERY
LONDON - - - ENGLAND
PRINTED IN ENGLAND

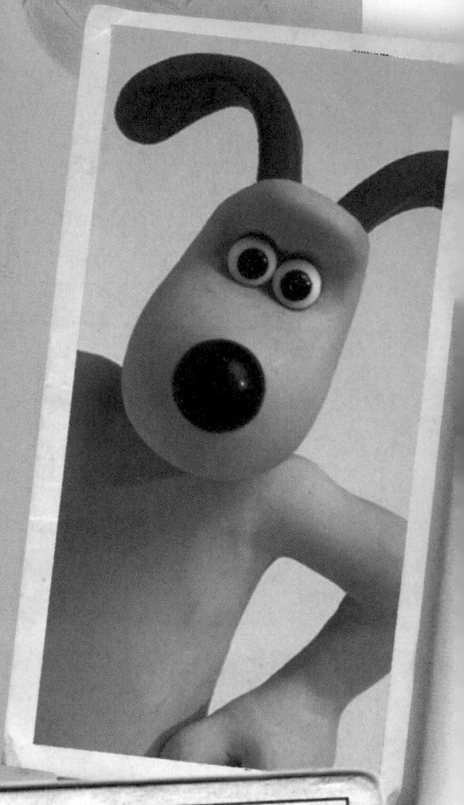

FOOTBALL

A SERIES OF 50

GROMIT

No. 2

The midfield maestro. Hard-working and doggedly determined. Always gets the crucial tackle in.

Issued by
CRACKING CONFECTIONERY
LONDON - - - ENGLAND
PRINTED IN ENGLAND

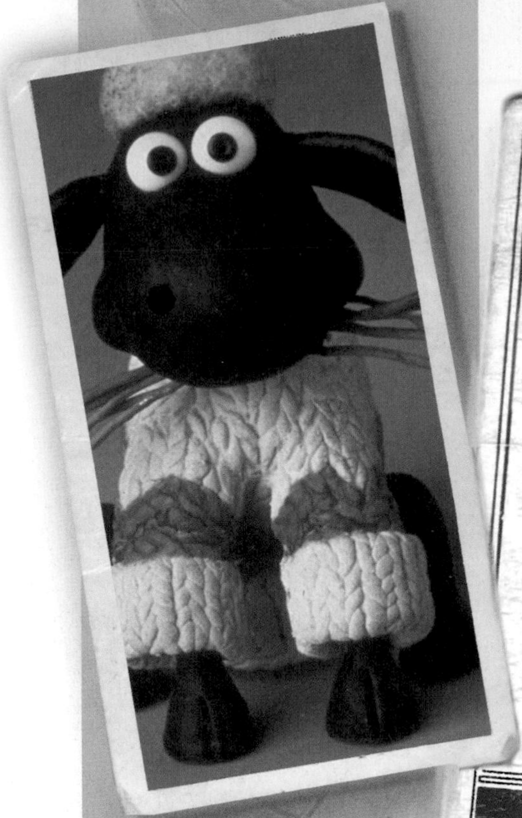

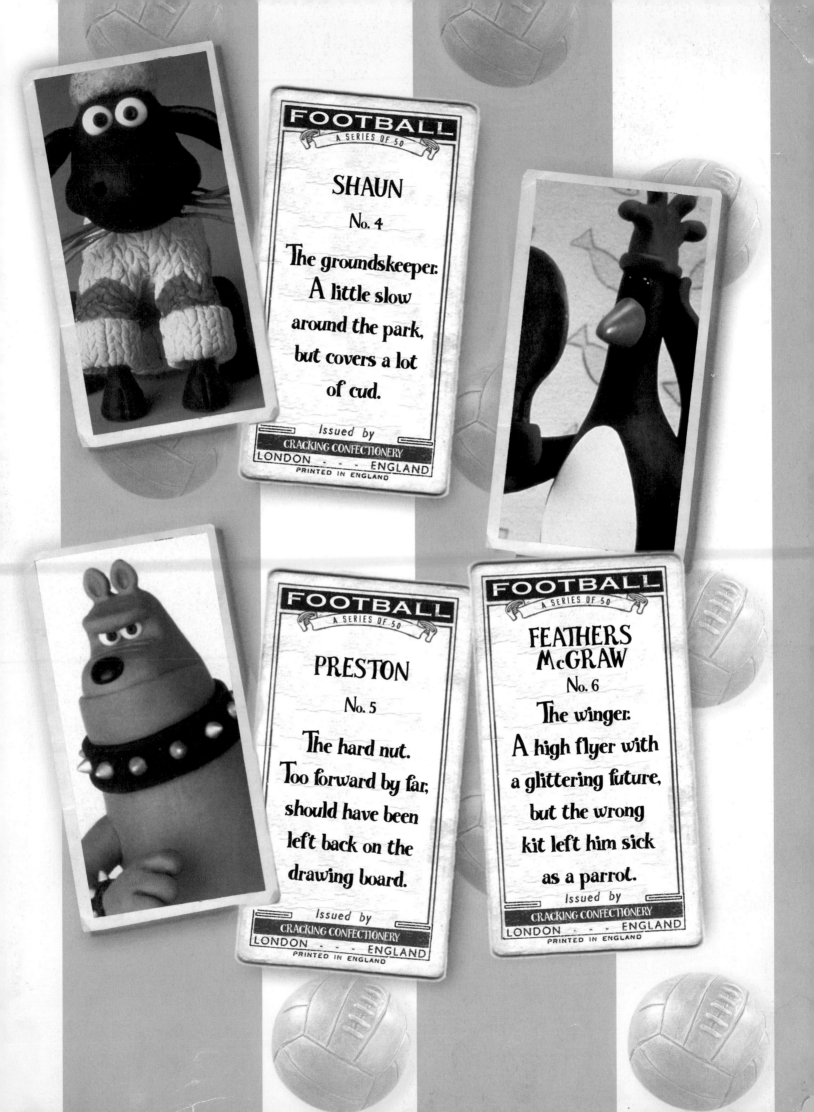

FOOTBALL

A SERIES OF 50

SHAUN

No. 4

The groundskeeper: A little slow around the park, but covers a lot of cud.

Issued by

CRACKING CONFECTIONERY

LONDON - - - ENGLAND

PRINTED IN ENGLAND

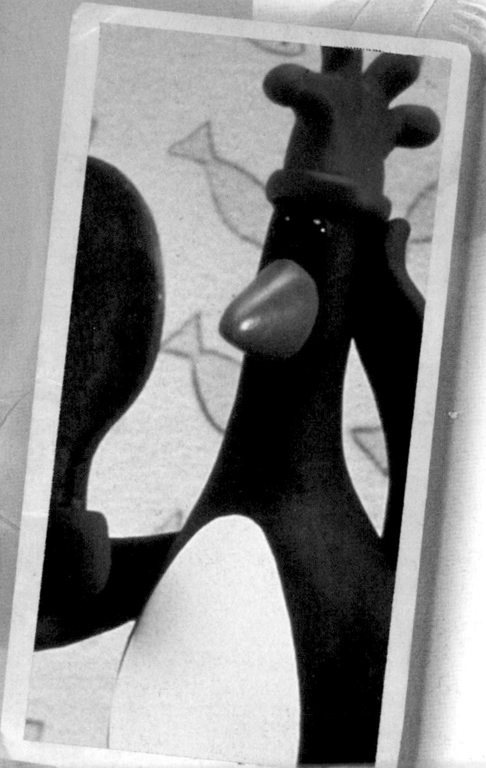

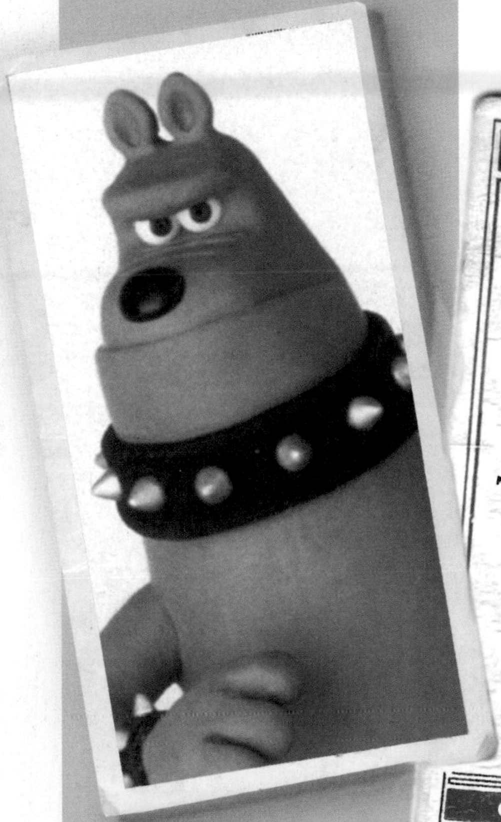

FOOTBALL

A SERIES OF 50

PRESTON

No. 5

The hard nut. Too forward by far; should have been left back on the drawing board.

Issued by

CRACKING CONFECTIONERY

LONDON - - - ENGLAND

PRINTED IN ENGLAND

FOOTBALL

A SERIES OF 50

FEATHERS McGRAW

No. 6

The winger: A high flyer with a glittering future, but the wrong kit left him sick as a parrot.

Issued by

CRACKING CONFECTIONERY

LONDON - - - ENGLAND

PRINTED IN ENGLAND

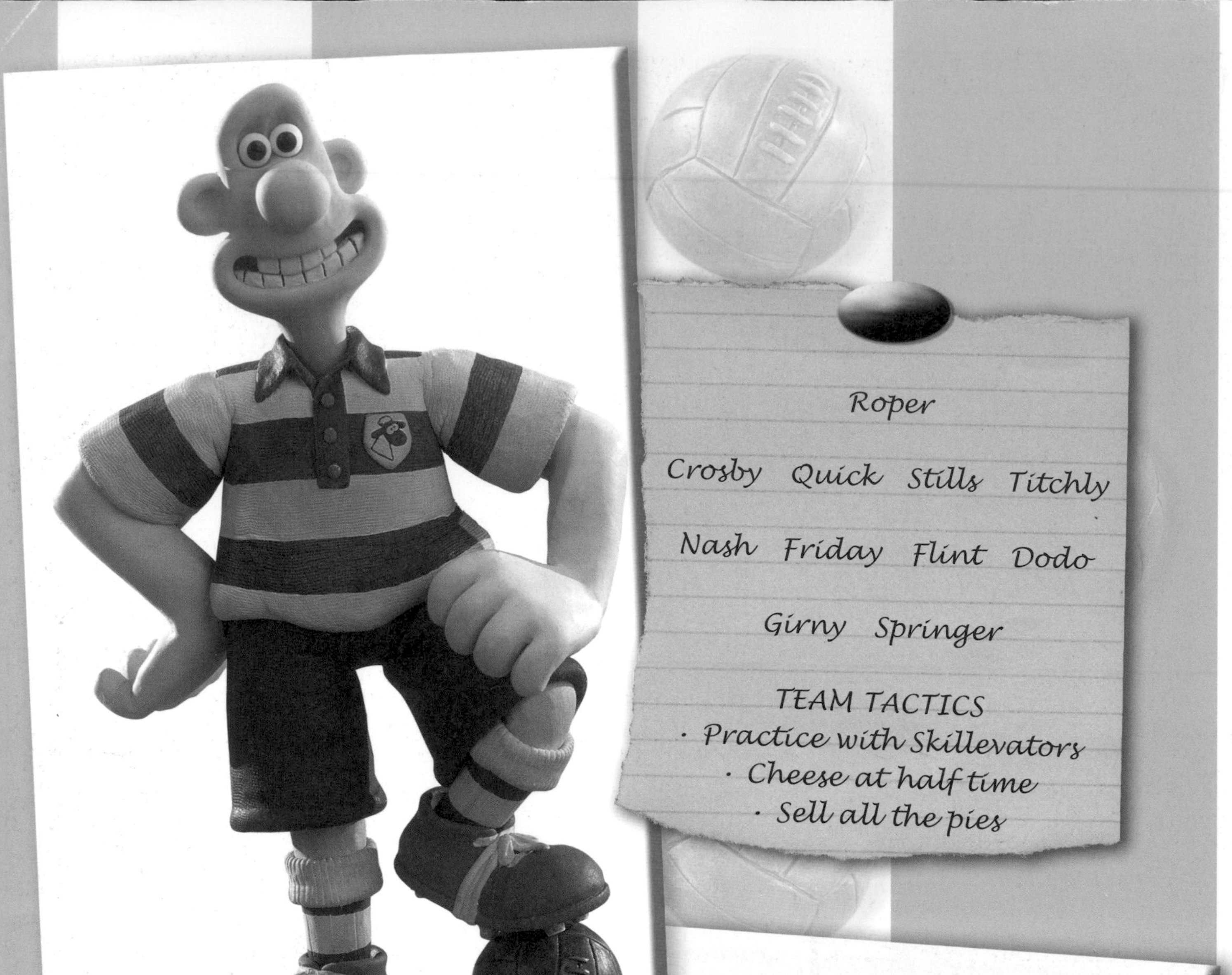

Roper

Crosby Quick Stills Titchly

Nash Friday Flint Dodo

Girny Springer

TEAM TACTICS

· Practice with Skillevators
· Cheese at half time
· Sell all the pies

TEAM TACTICS

· Forget Skillevators
· Crackers at half time
· Sell Bill

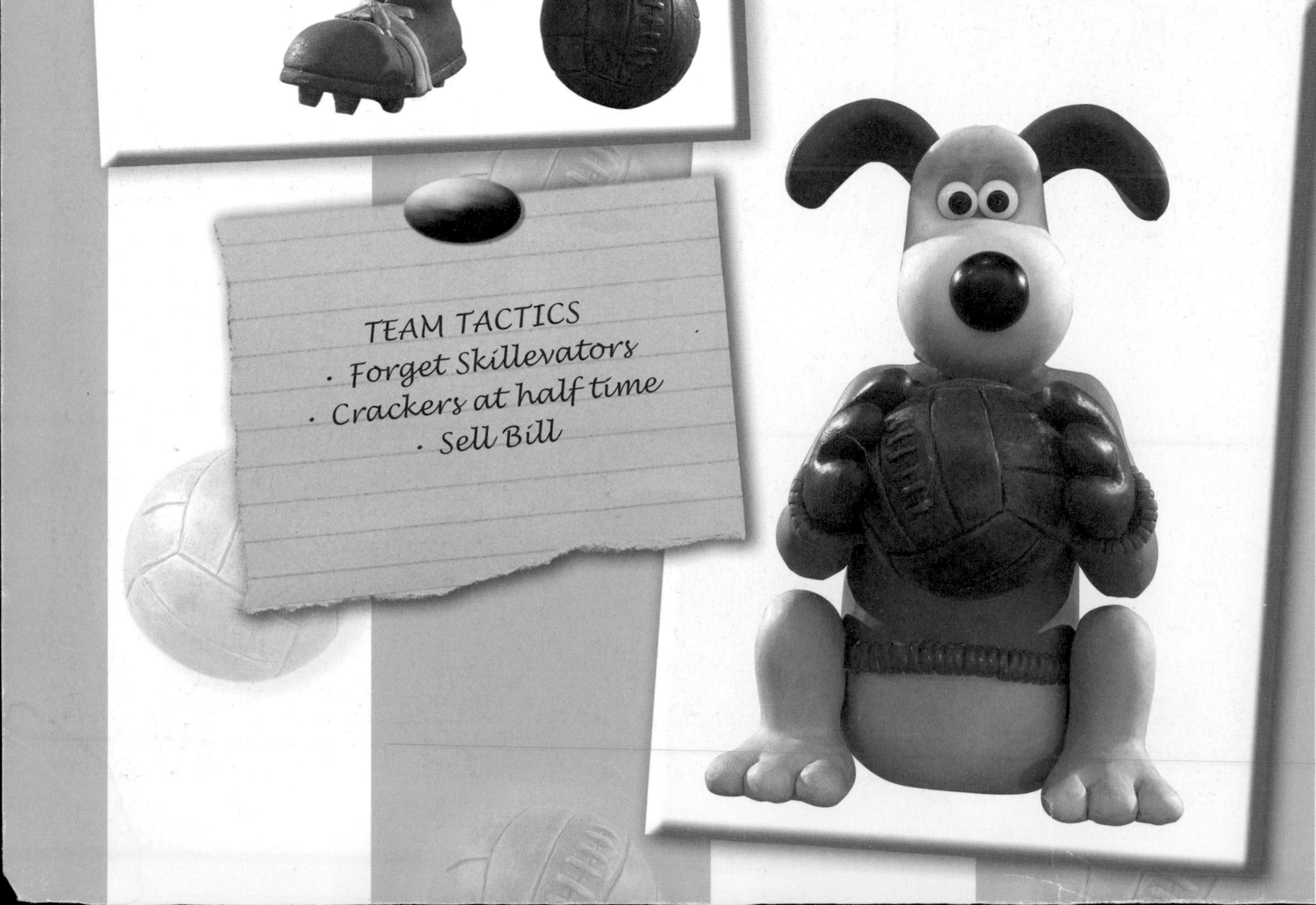

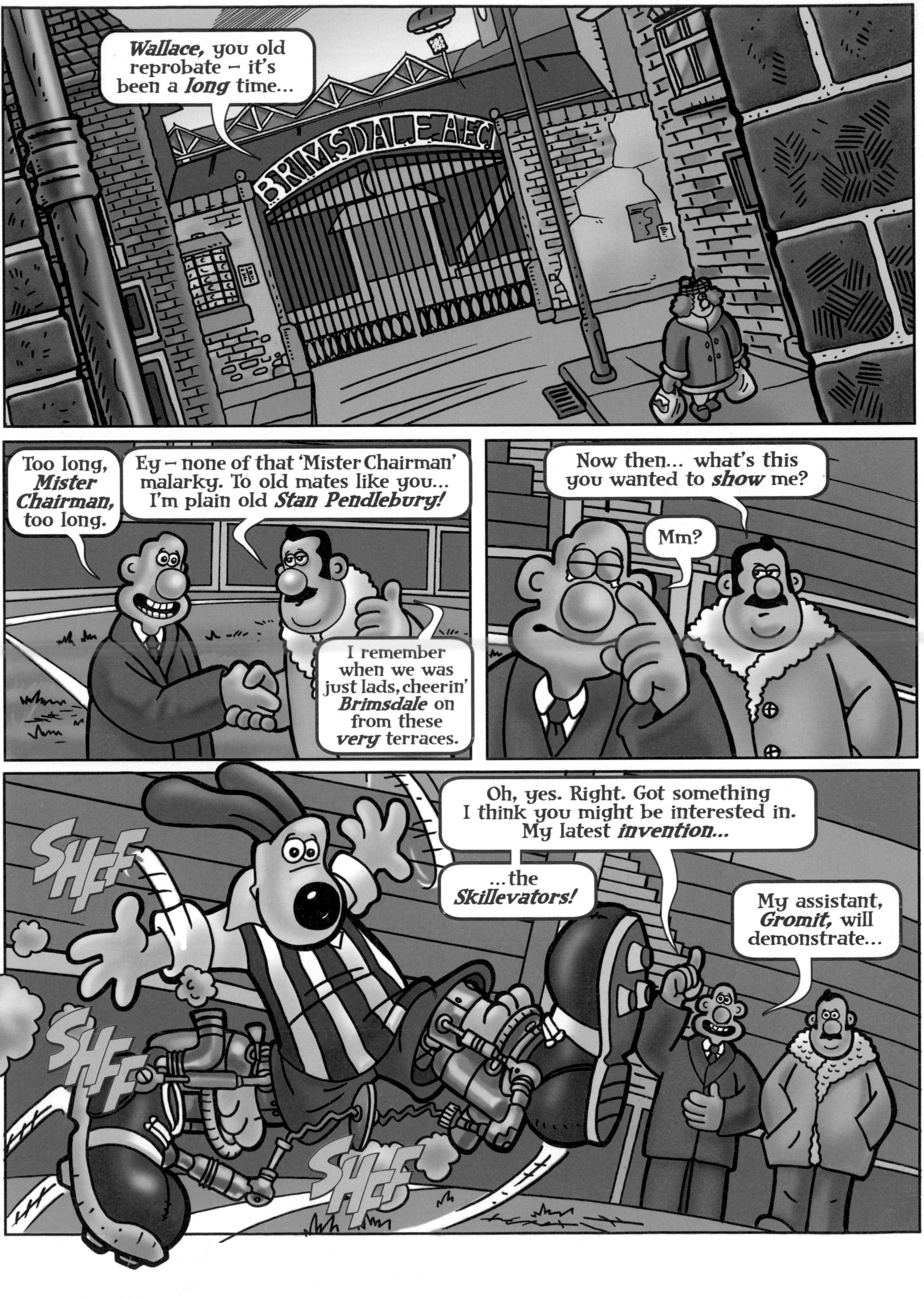
Wallace, you old reprobate – it's been a long time...
BRIMSDALE A.F.C.
Too long, Mister Chairman, too long.
Ey – none of that 'Mister Chairman' malarky. To old mates like you... I'm plain old Stan Pendlebury!
I remember when we was just lads, cheerin' Brimsdale on from these very terraces.
Now then... what's this you wanted to show me?
Mm?
Oh, yes. Right. Got something I think you might be interested in. My latest invention...
...the Skillevators!
My assistant, Gromit, will demonstrate...
SHFF
SHFF
SHFF

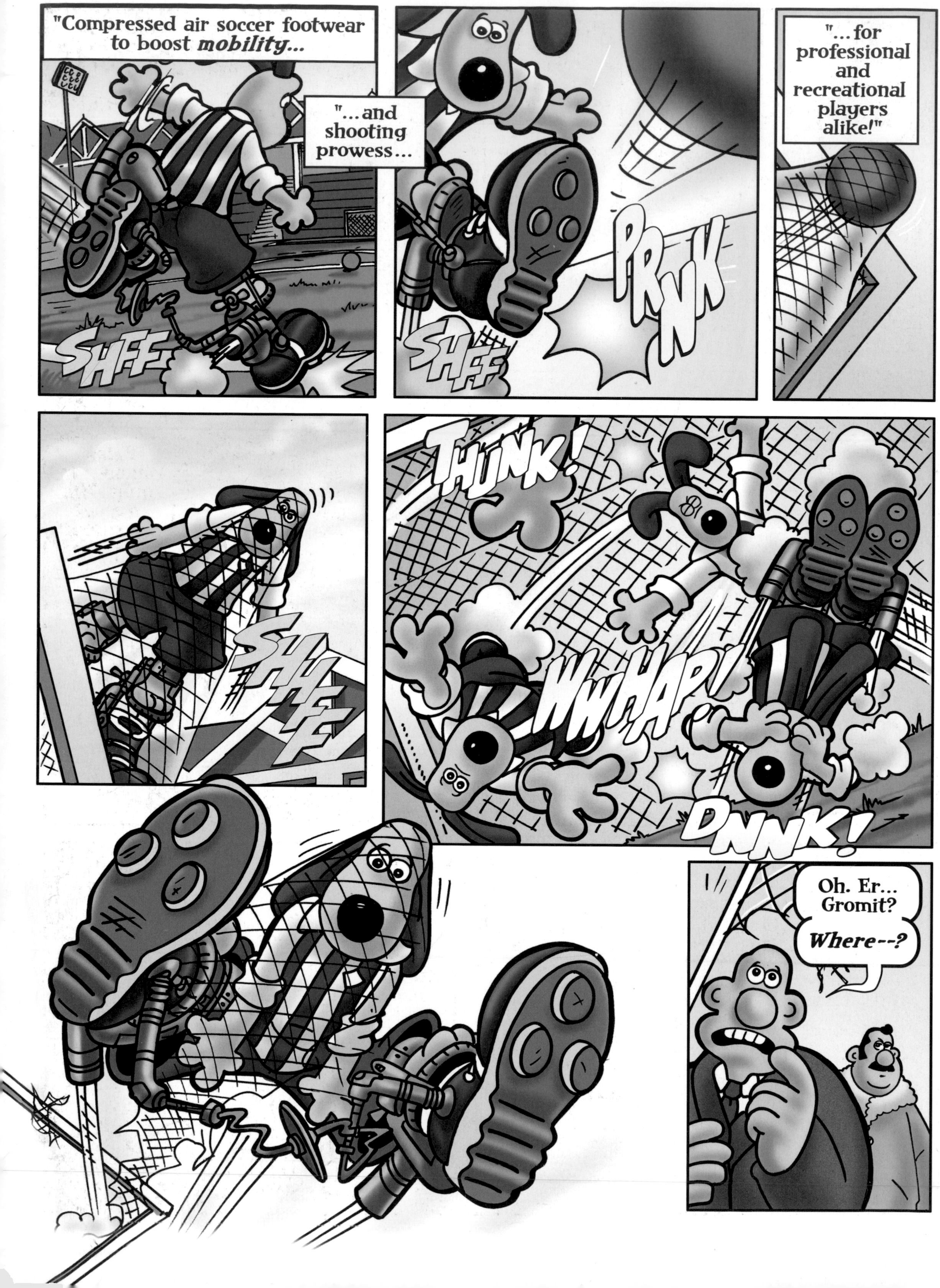
"Compressed air soccer footwear to boost *mobility*...
"...and shooting prowess...
SHFF
SHFF
PRNK
"...for professional and recreational players alike!"
SHFF
THUNK!
WWHAP!
DNNK!
Oh. Er... Gromit?
Where--?

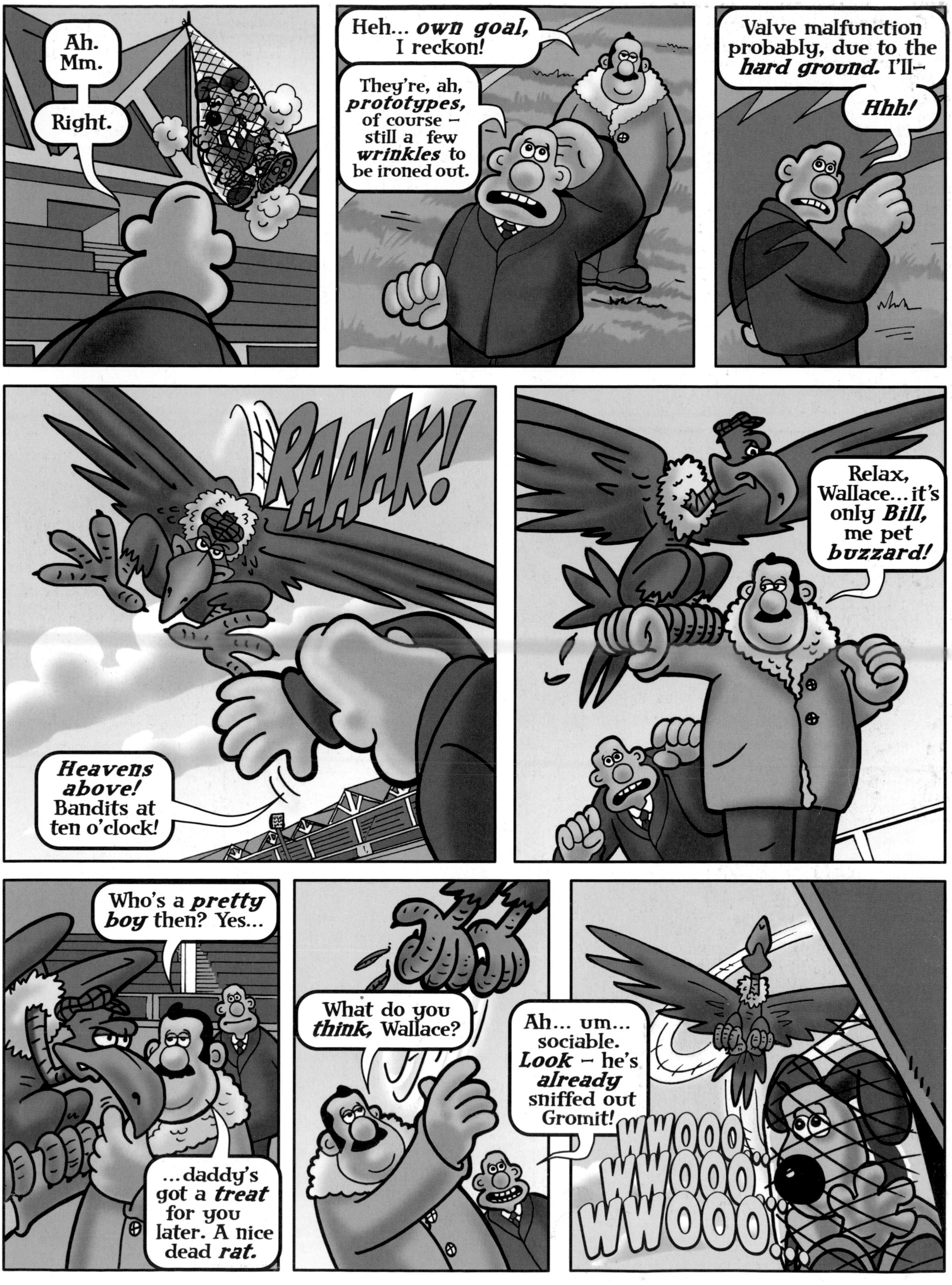
Ah. Mm.
Right.
Heh... own goal, I reckon!
They're, ah, prototypes, of course – still a few wrinkles to be ironed out.
Valve malfunction probably, due to the hard ground. I'll–
Hhh!
RAAAK!
Heavens above! Bandits at ten o'clock!
Relax, Wallace... it's only Bill, me pet buzzard!
Who's a pretty boy then? Yes...
...daddy's got a treat for you later. A nice dead rat.
What do you think, Wallace?
Ah... um... sociable. Look – he's already sniffed out Gromit!
WWOOO... WWOOO... WWOOO...

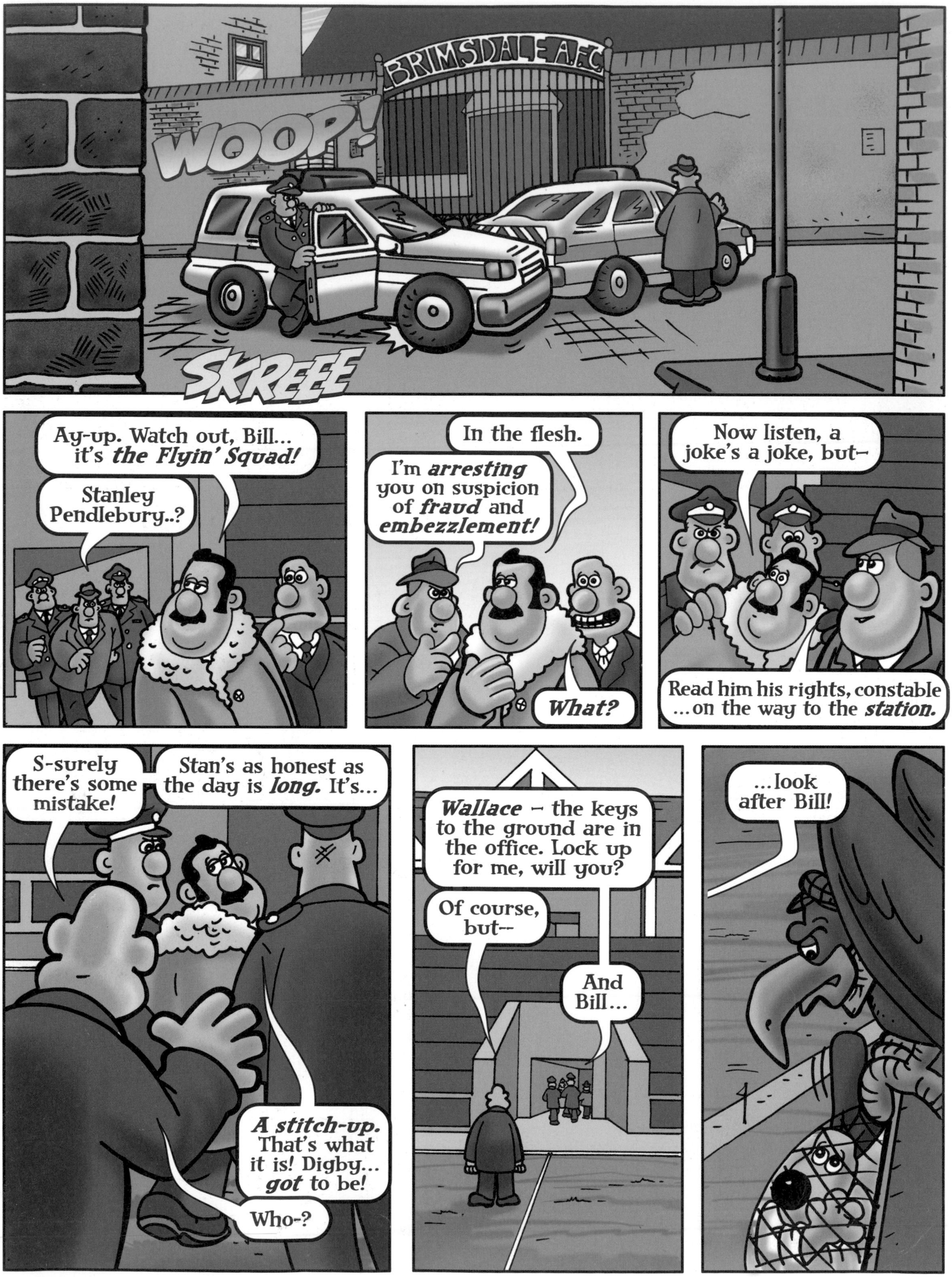
BRIMSDALE A.F.C.
WOOP!
SKREEE
Ay-up. Watch out, Bill... it's *the Flyin' Squad!*
Stanley Pendlebury..?
In the flesh.
I'm *arresting* you on suspicion of *fraud* and *embezzlement!*
What?
Now listen, a joke's a joke, but–
Read him his rights, constable ...on the way to the *station.*
S-surely there's some mistake!
Stan's as honest as the day is *long.* It's...
A stitch-up. That's what it is! Digby... *got* to be!
Who-?
Wallace – the keys to the ground are in the office. Lock up for me, will you?
Of course, but--
And Bill...
...look after Bill!

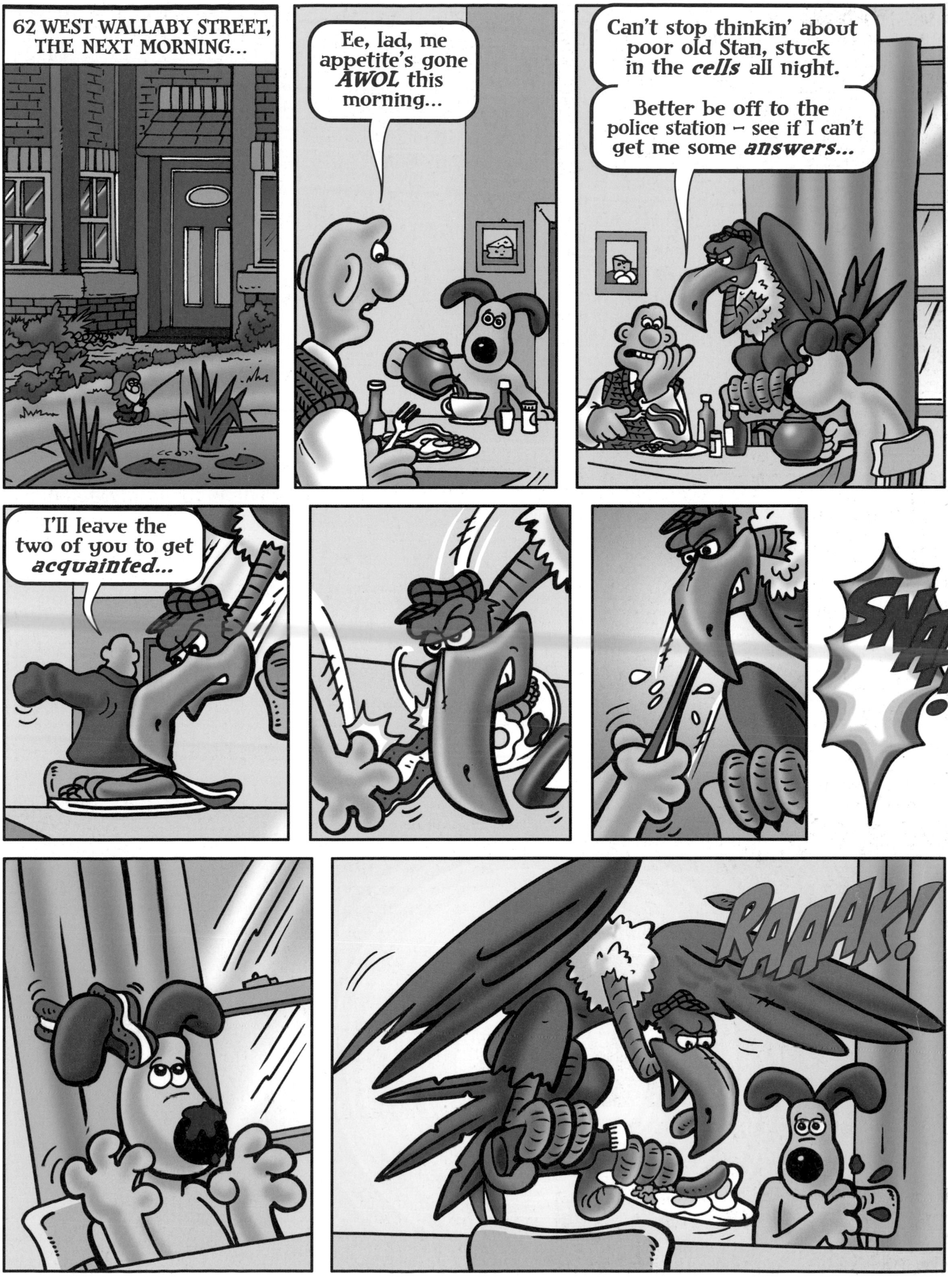
62 WEST WALLABY STREET, THE NEXT MORNING...
Ee, lad, me appetite's gone AWOL this morning...
Can't stop thinkin' about poor old Stan, stuck in the cells all night.
Better be off to the police station – see if I can't get me some answers...
I'll leave the two of you to get acquainted...
SNAP!
RAAAK!

SHORTLY, AT THE POLICE STATION...

Wallace! Sorry to keep you waiting... I was just finishin' up me *breakfast.*

Condemned man, hearty meal... you know the score.

Mm. Got to keep your strength up, I suppose.

You seem... *cheerful,* all things considered.

Ah, well. Had *time* to gather me thoughts, haven't I...?

...put my, ah, *hosts* onto the real culprit – that thievin' rat, Digby Hedgerow!

Digby... Hedgerow?

Partners we were... each of us with a fifty percent share in Brimsdale...

"Top bloke on the surface... but he was *cookin' the books,* pocketin' a slice of the gate-money every matchday."

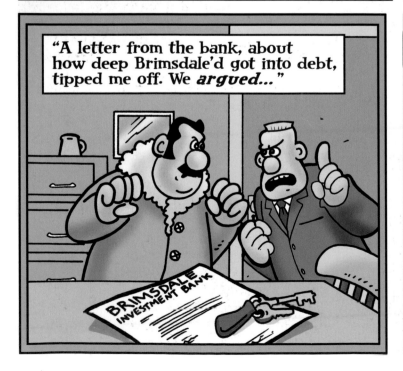

"A letter from the bank, about how deep Brimsdale'd got into debt, tipped me off. We *argued...*"

BRIMSDALE INVESTMENT BANK

...an' next thing I know, he's *disappeared,* gone underground, leavin' me squarely in the *frame* for all *his* dirty work.

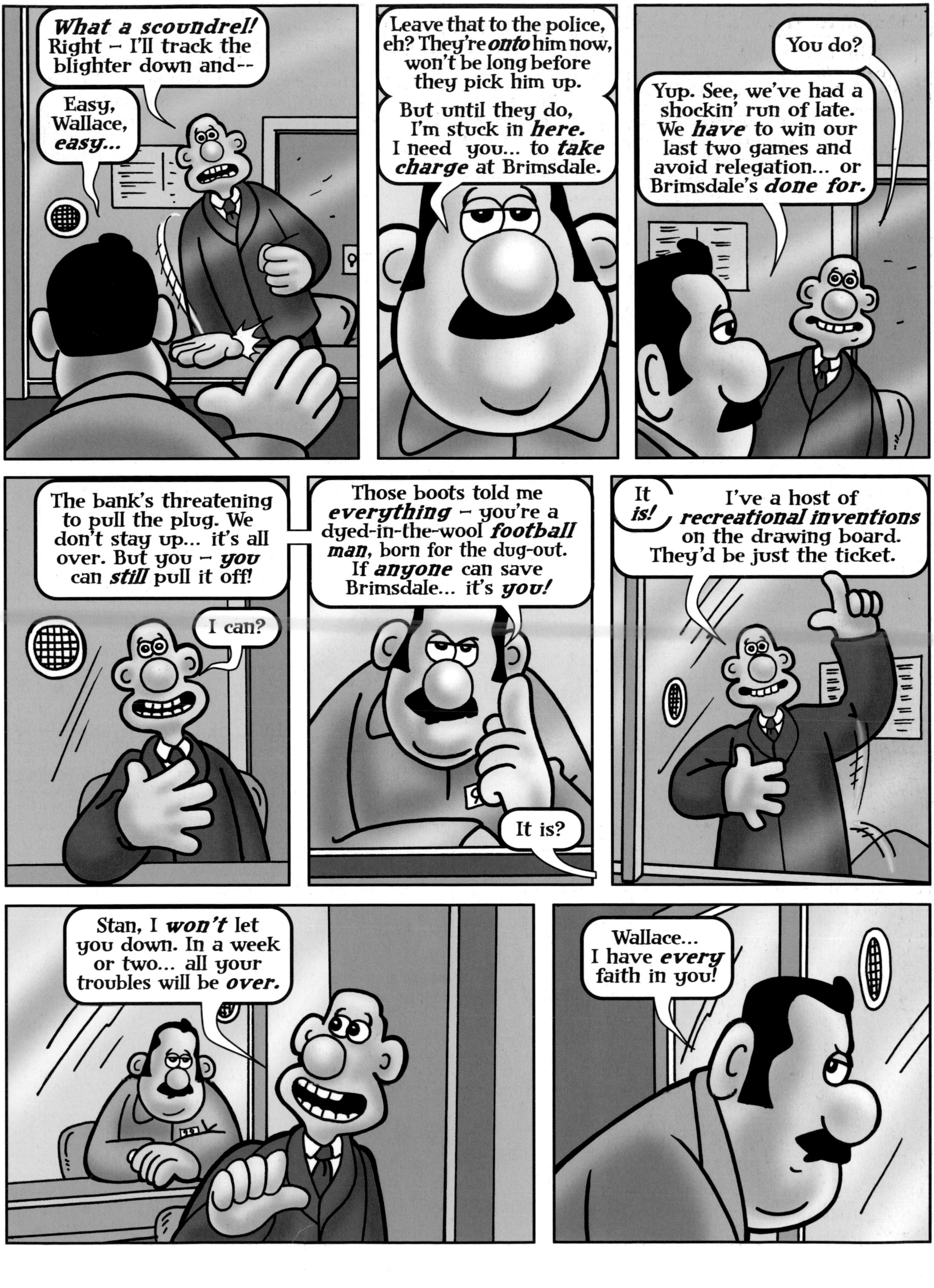
What a scoundrel! Right – I'll track the blighter down and--
Easy, Wallace, easy...
Leave that to the police, eh? They're onto him now, won't be long before they pick him up.
But until they do, I'm stuck in here. I need you... to take charge at Brimsdale.
You do?
Yup. See, we've had a shockin' run of late. We have to win our last two games and avoid relegation... or Brimsdale's done for.
The bank's threatening to pull the plug. We don't stay up... it's all over. But you – you can still pull it off!
Those boots told me everything – you're a dyed-in-the-wool football man, born for the dug-out. If anyone can save Brimsdale... it's you!
I can?
It is?
It is!
I've a host of recreational inventions on the drawing board. They'd be just the ticket.
Stan, I won't let you down. In a week or two... all your troubles will be over.
Wallace... I have every faith in you!

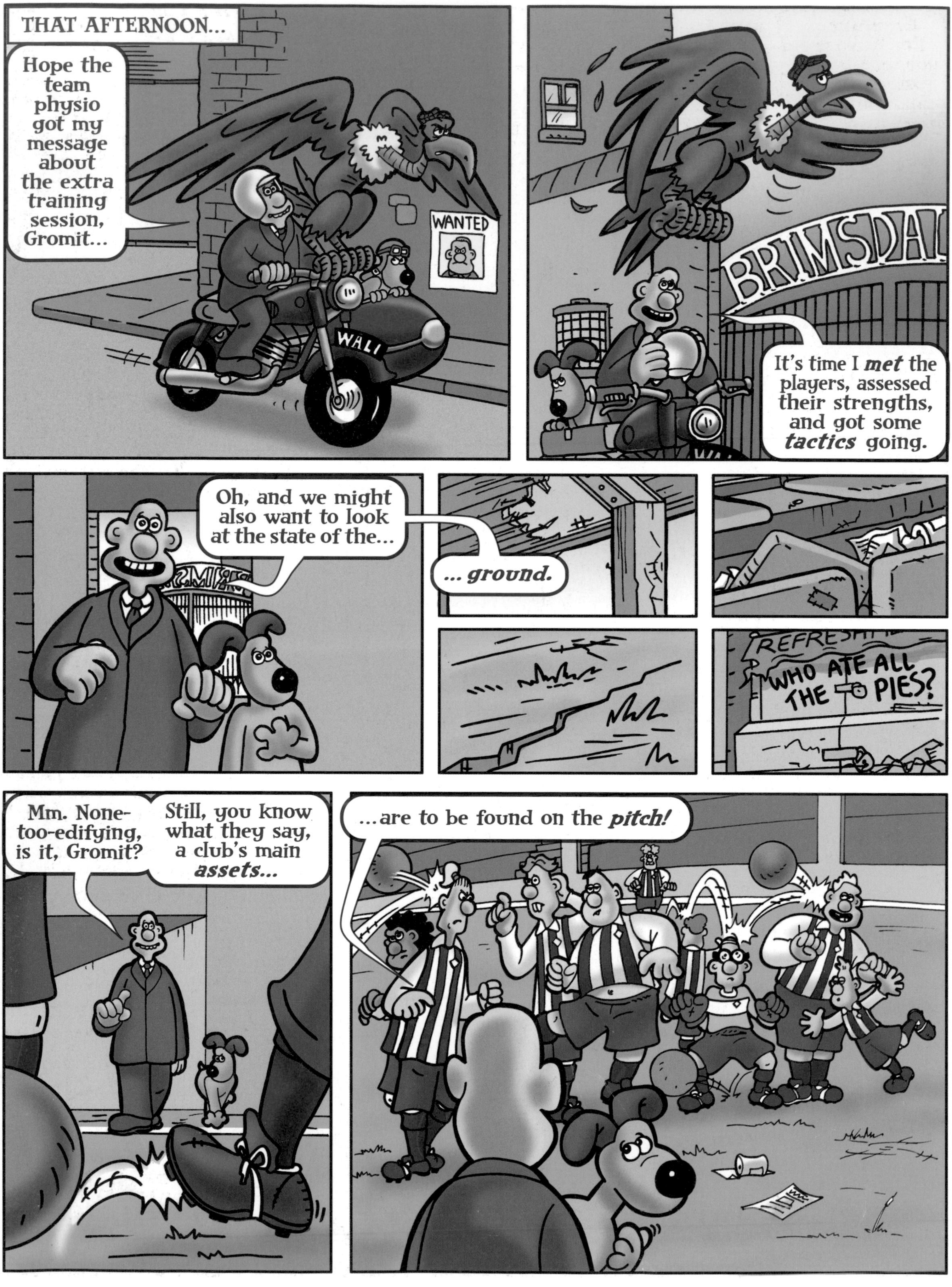
THAT AFTERNOON...
Hope the team physio got my message about the extra training session, Gromit...
WANTED
WALI
It's time I *met* the players, assessed their strengths, and got some *tactics* going.
BRIMSDAL
Oh, and we might also want to look at the state of the...
... ground.
REFRESH
WHO ATE ALL THE PIES?
Mm. None-too-edifying, is it, Gromit?
Still, you know what they say, a club's main *assets...*
...are to be found on the *pitch!*

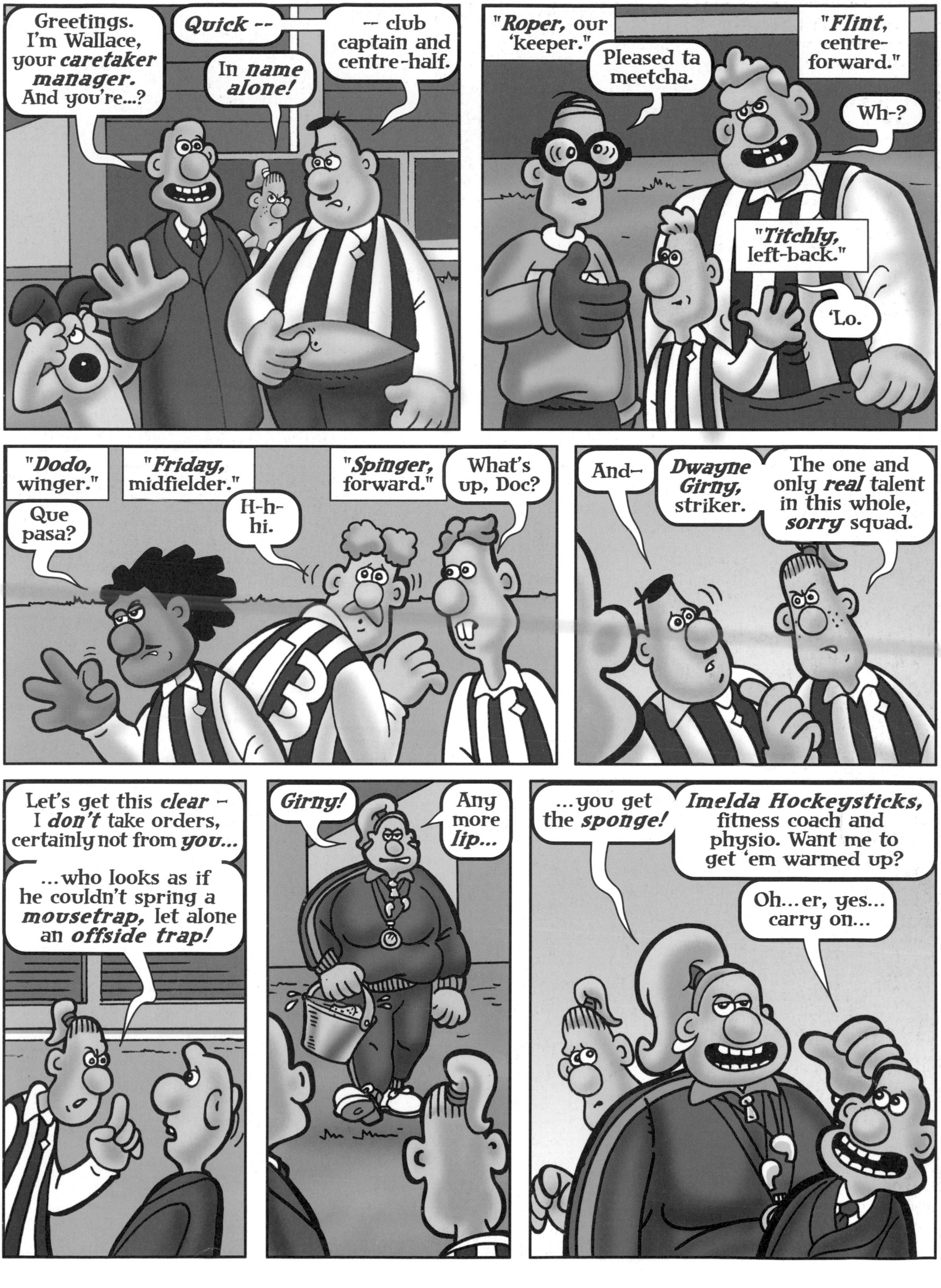
Greetings. I'm Wallace, your *caretaker manager.* And you're...?
Quick --
In *name alone!*
-- club captain and centre-half.
"*Roper,* our 'keeper."
Pleased ta meetcha.
"*Flint,* centre-forward."
Wh-?
"*Titchly,* left-back."
'Lo.
"*Dodo,* winger."
Que pasa?
"*Friday,* midfielder."
H-h-hi.
"*Spinger,* forward."
What's up, Doc?
And–
Dwayne Girny, striker.
The one and only *real* talent in this whole, *sorry* squad.
Let's get this *clear* – I *don't* take orders, certainly not from *you...*
...who looks as if he couldn't spring a *mousetrap,* let alone an *offside trap!*
Girny!
Any more *lip...*
...you get the *sponge!*
Imelda Hockeysticks, fitness coach and physio. Want me to get 'em warmed up?
Oh...er, yes... carry on...

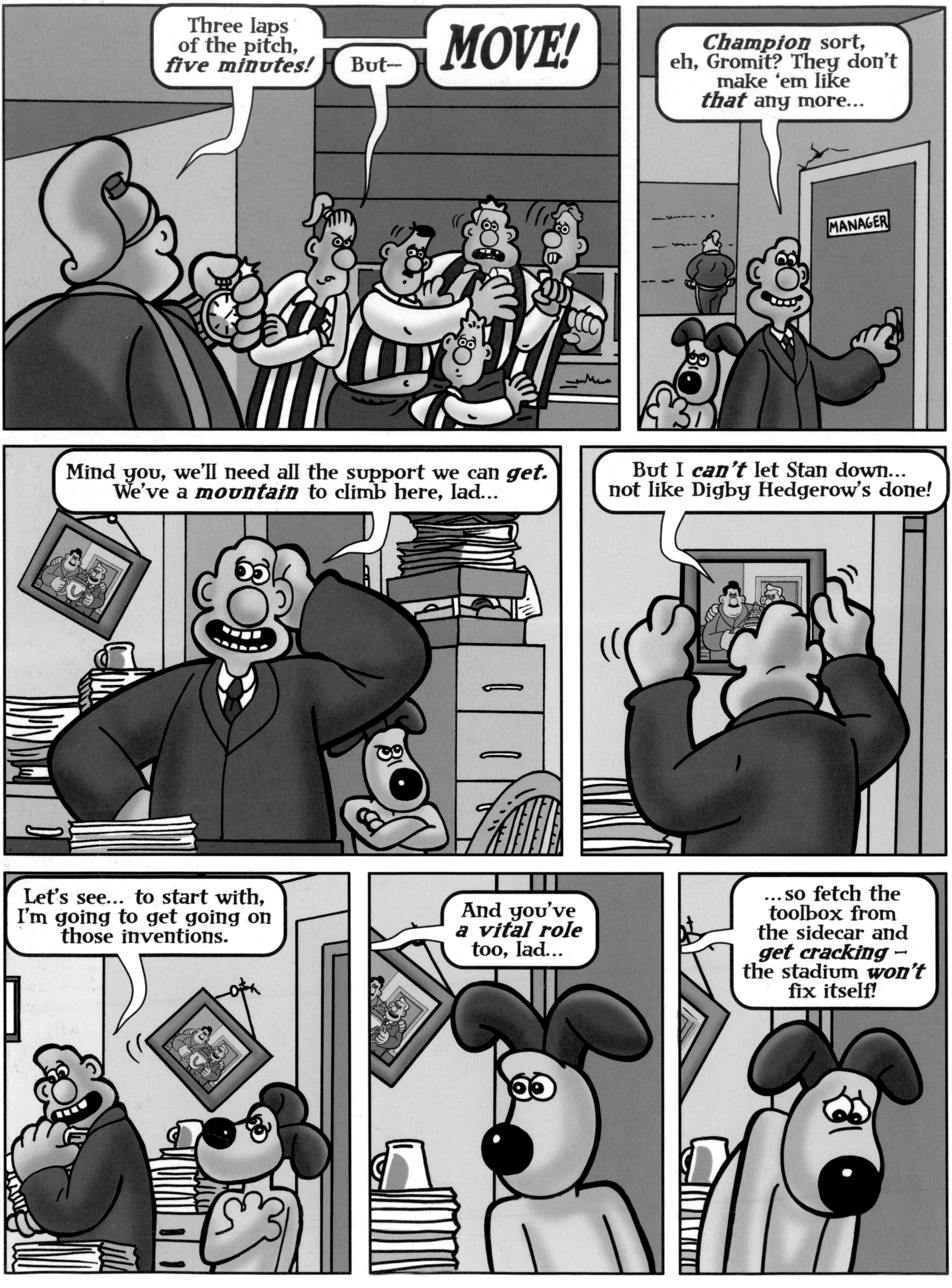
Three laps of the pitch, *five minutes!*
But--
MOVE!
Champion sort, eh, Gromit? They don't make 'em like *that* any more...
MANAGER
Mind you, we'll need all the support we can *get.* We've a *mountain* to climb here, lad...
But I *can't* let Stan down... not like Digby Hedgerow's done!
Let's see... to start with, I'm going to get going on those inventions.
And you've *a vital role* too, lad...
...so fetch the toolbox from the sidecar and *get cracking* – the stadium *won't* fix itself!

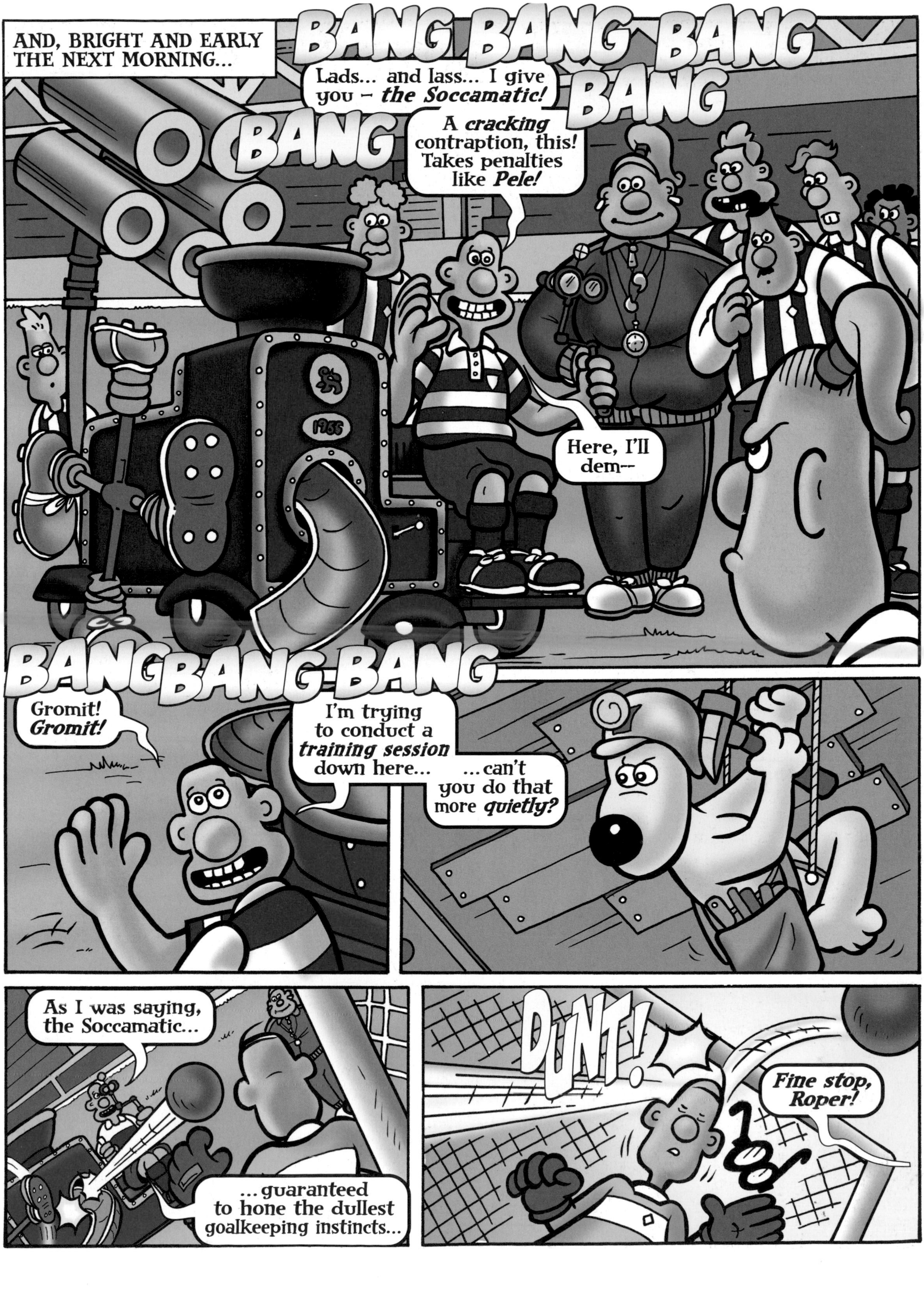

AND, BRIGHT AND EARLY THE NEXT MORNING...
BANG BANG BANG
BANG
Lads... and lass... I give you – *the Soccamatic!*
BANG
A *cracking* contraption, this! Takes penalties like *Pele!*
1966
Here, I'll dem--
BANG BANG BANG
Gromit! *Gromit!*
I'm trying to conduct a *training session* down here...
...can't you do that more *quietly?*
As I was saying, the Soccamatic...
...guaranteed to hone the dullest goalkeeping instincts...
DUNT!
Fine stop, Roper!

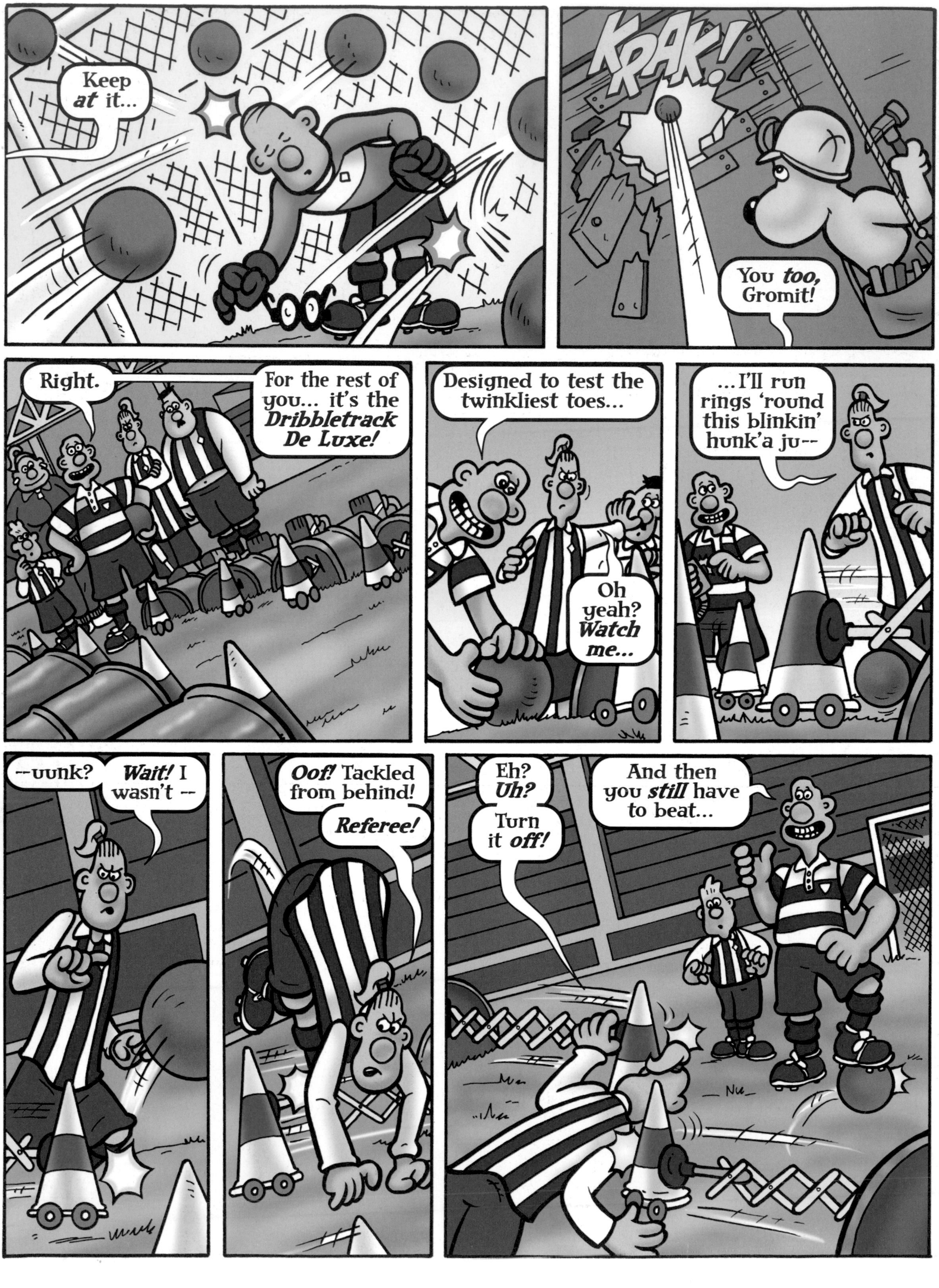
Keep *at* it...
KRAK!
You *too,* Gromit!
Right.
For the rest of you... it's the *Dribbletrack De Luxe!*
Designed to test the twinkliest toes...
Oh yeah? *Watch me...*
...I'll run rings 'round this blinkin' hunk'a ju--
--uunk?
Wait! I wasn't --
Oof! Tackled from behind!
Referee!
Eh? *Uh?*
Turn it *off!*
And then you *still* have to beat...

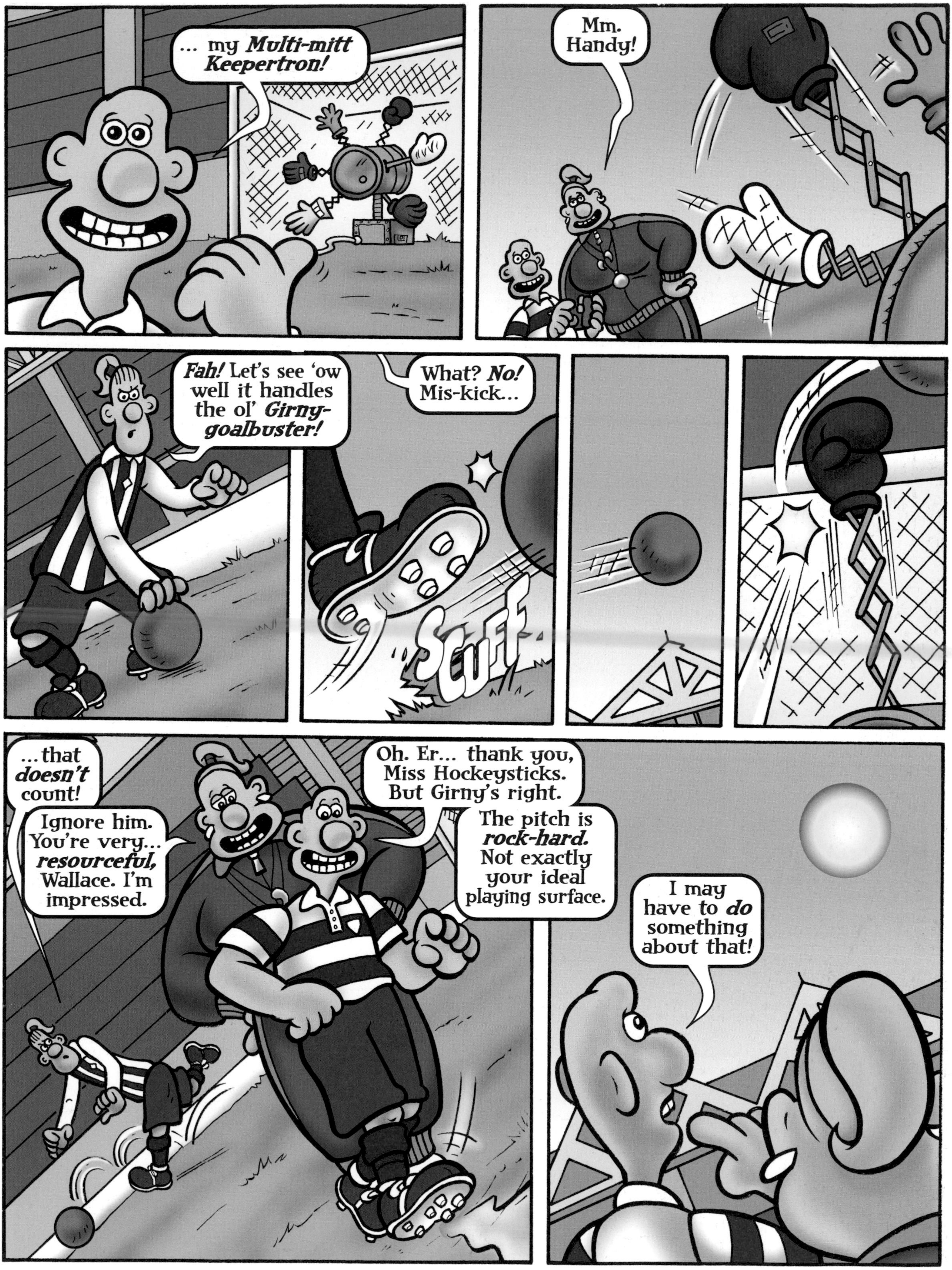

... my Multi-mitt Keepertron!
Mm. Handy!
Fah! Let's see 'ow well it handles the ol' Girny-goalbuster!
What? No! Mis-kick...
SCUFF
...that doesn't count!
Ignore him. You're very... resourceful, Wallace. I'm impressed.
Oh. Er... thank you, Miss Hockeysticks. But Girny's right.
The pitch is rock-hard. Not exactly your ideal playing surface.
I may have to do something about that!

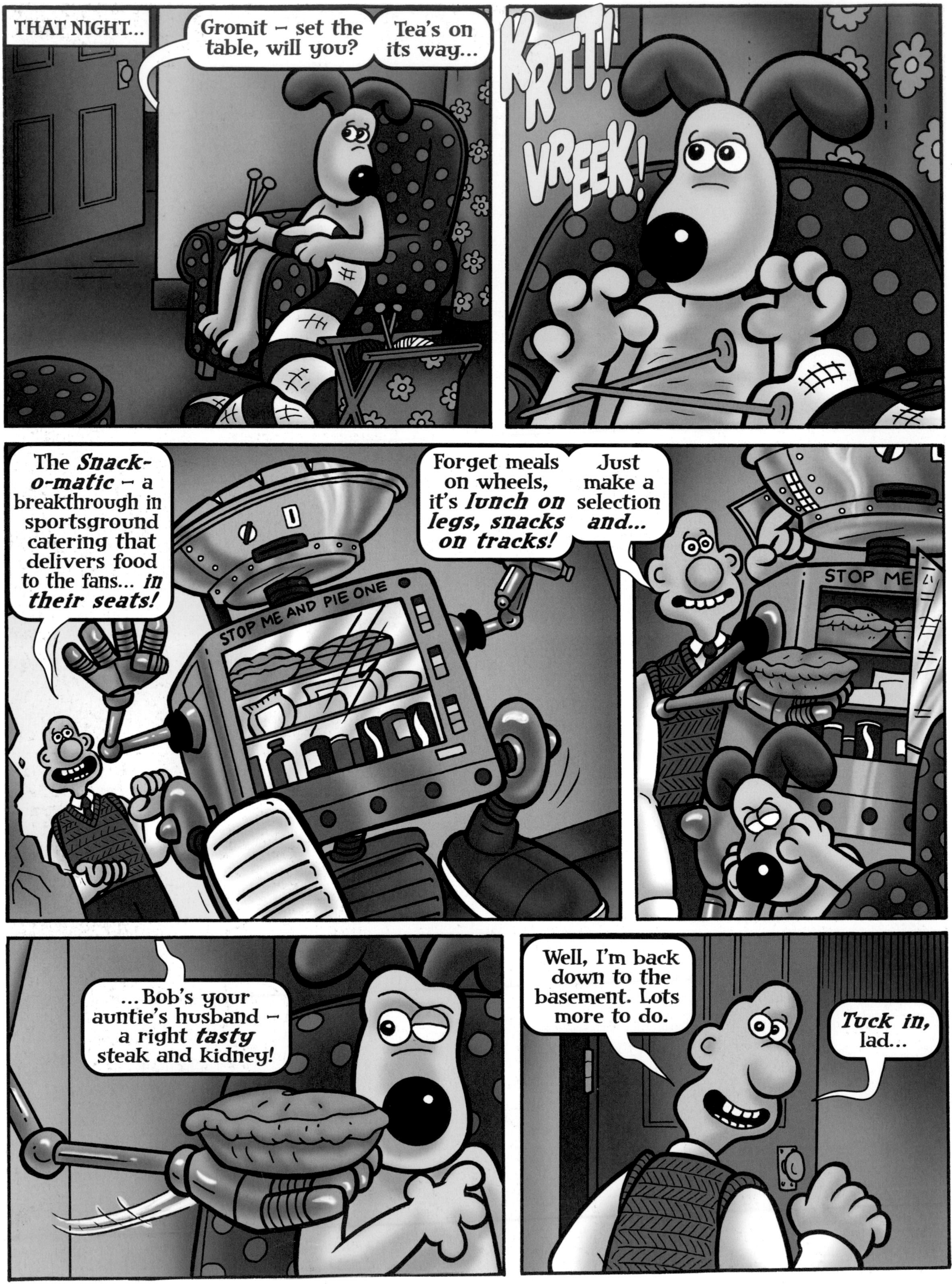
THAT NIGHT...
Gromit – set the table, will you?
Tea's on its way...
KRTT!
VREEK!
The *Snack-o-matic* – a breakthrough in sportsground catering that delivers food to the fans... *in their seats!*
STOP ME AND PIE ONE
Forget meals on wheels, it's *lunch on legs, snacks on tracks!*
Just make a selection and...
STOP ME
...Bob's your auntie's husband – a right *tasty* steak and kidney!
Well, I'm back down to the basement. Lots more to do.
Tuck in, lad...

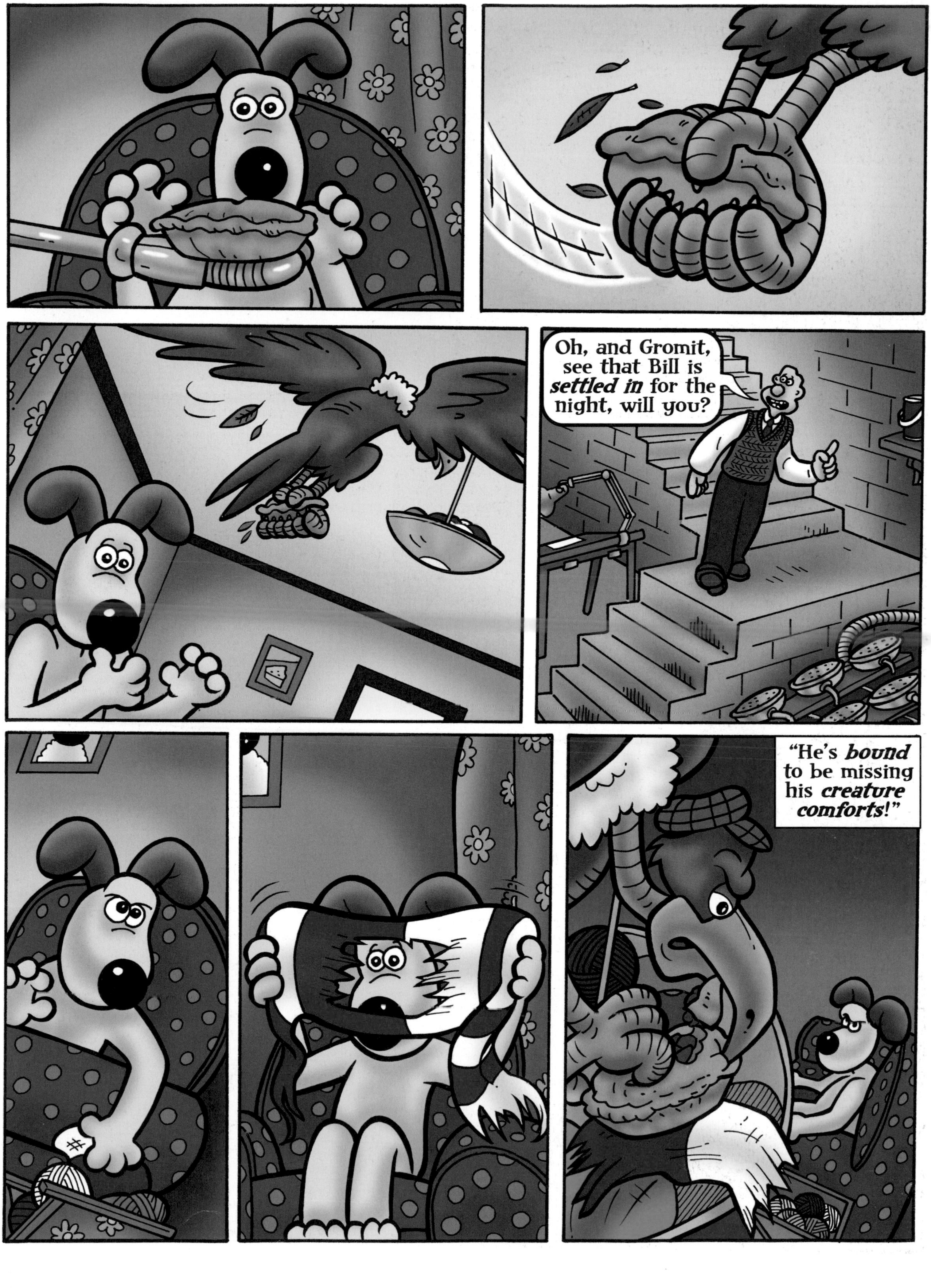
Oh, and Gromit, see that Bill is *settled in* for the night, will you?
"He's *bound* to be missing his *creature comforts*!"

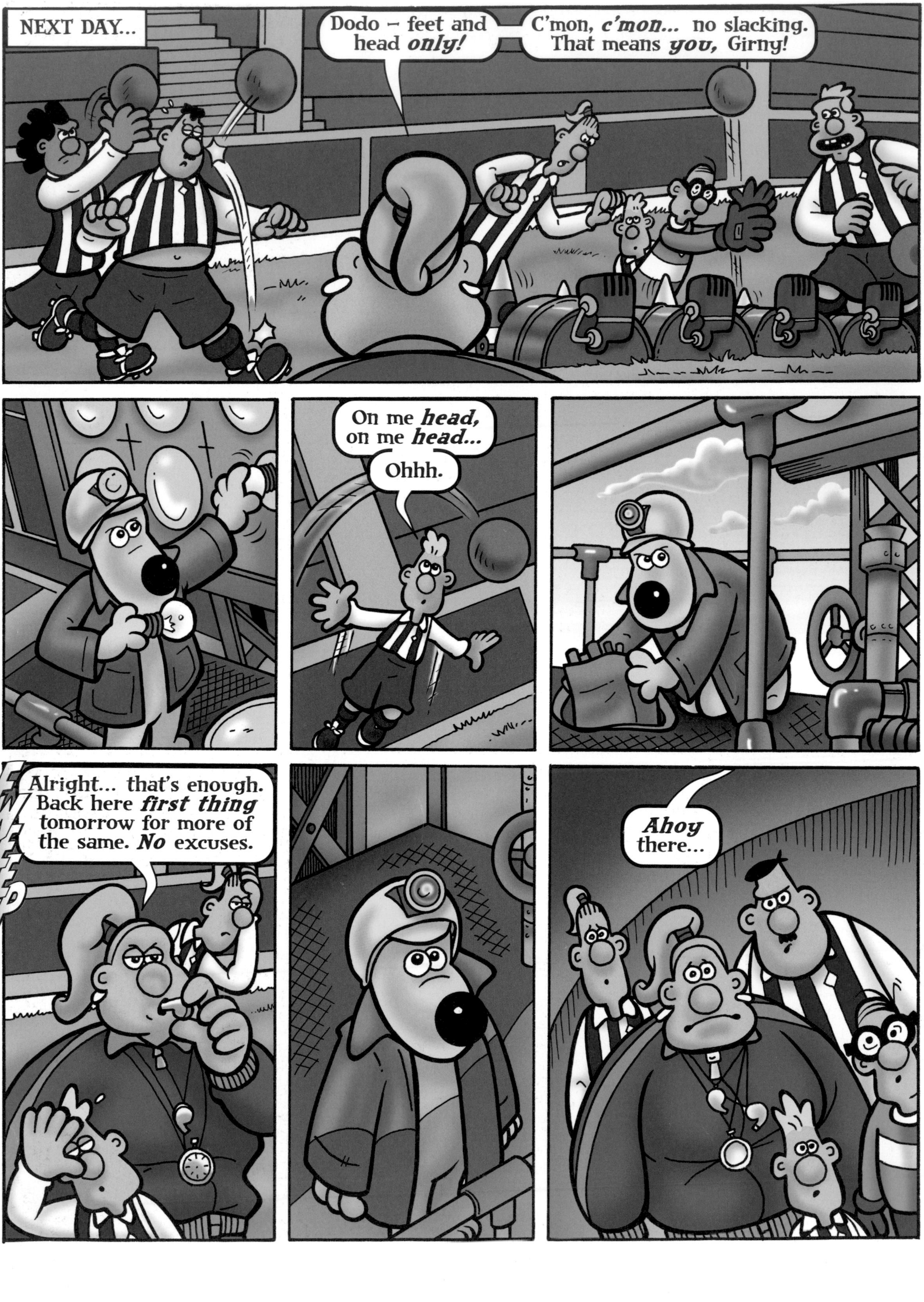
NEXT DAY...
Dodo – feet and head *only!*
C'mon, *c'mon...* no slacking. That means *you,* Girny!
On me *head,* on me *head...*
Ohhh.
FWEEP
Alright... that's enough. Back here *first thing* tomorrow for more of the same. *No* excuses.
Ahoy there...

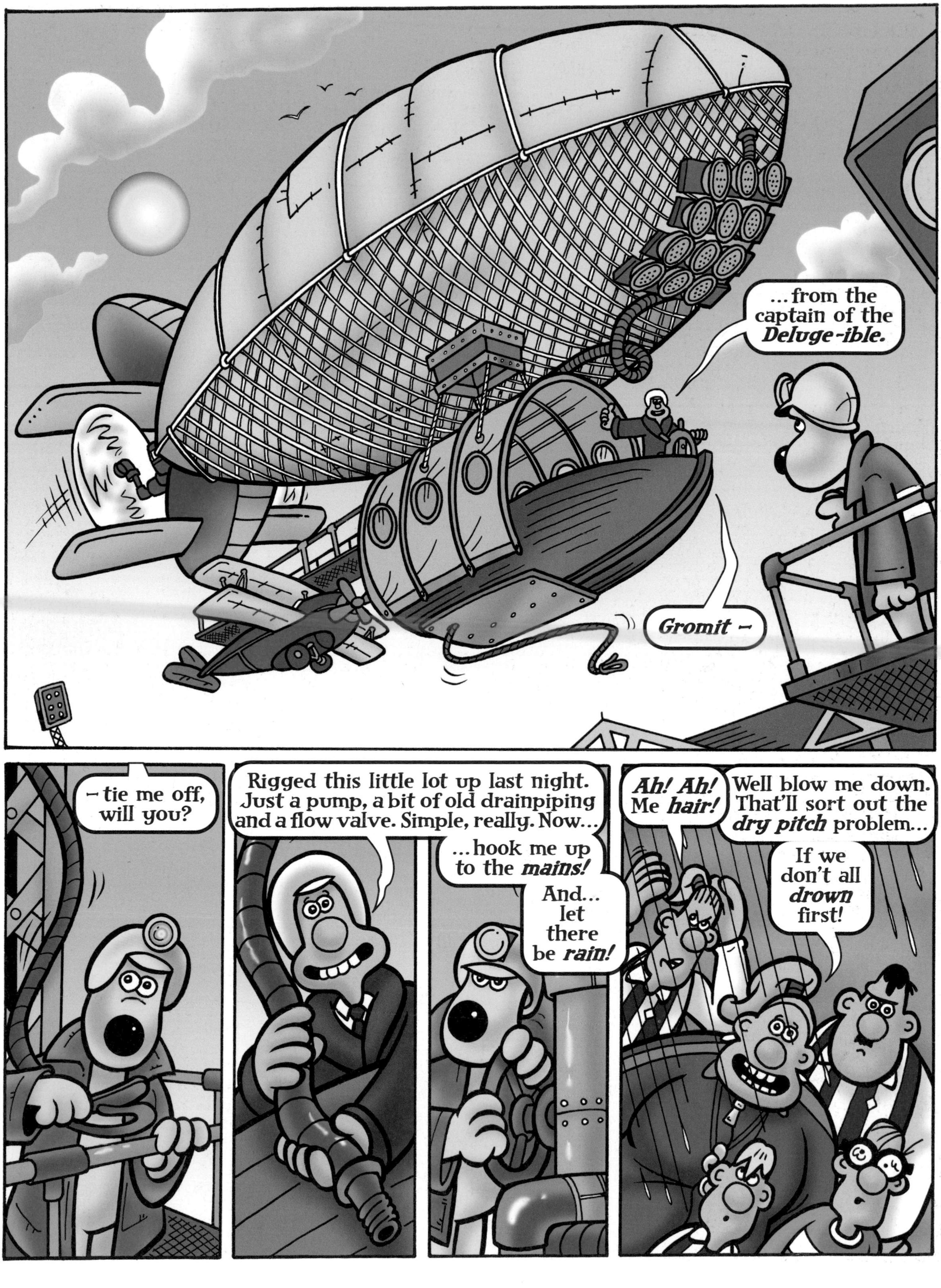
...from the captain of the *Deluge-ible.*
Gromit –
– tie me off, will you?
Rigged this little lot up last night. Just a pump, a bit of old drainpiping and a flow valve. Simple, really. Now...
...hook me up to the *mains!*
And... let there be *rain!*
Ah! Ah! Me *hair!*
Well blow me down. That'll sort out the *dry pitch* problem...
If we don't all *drown* first!

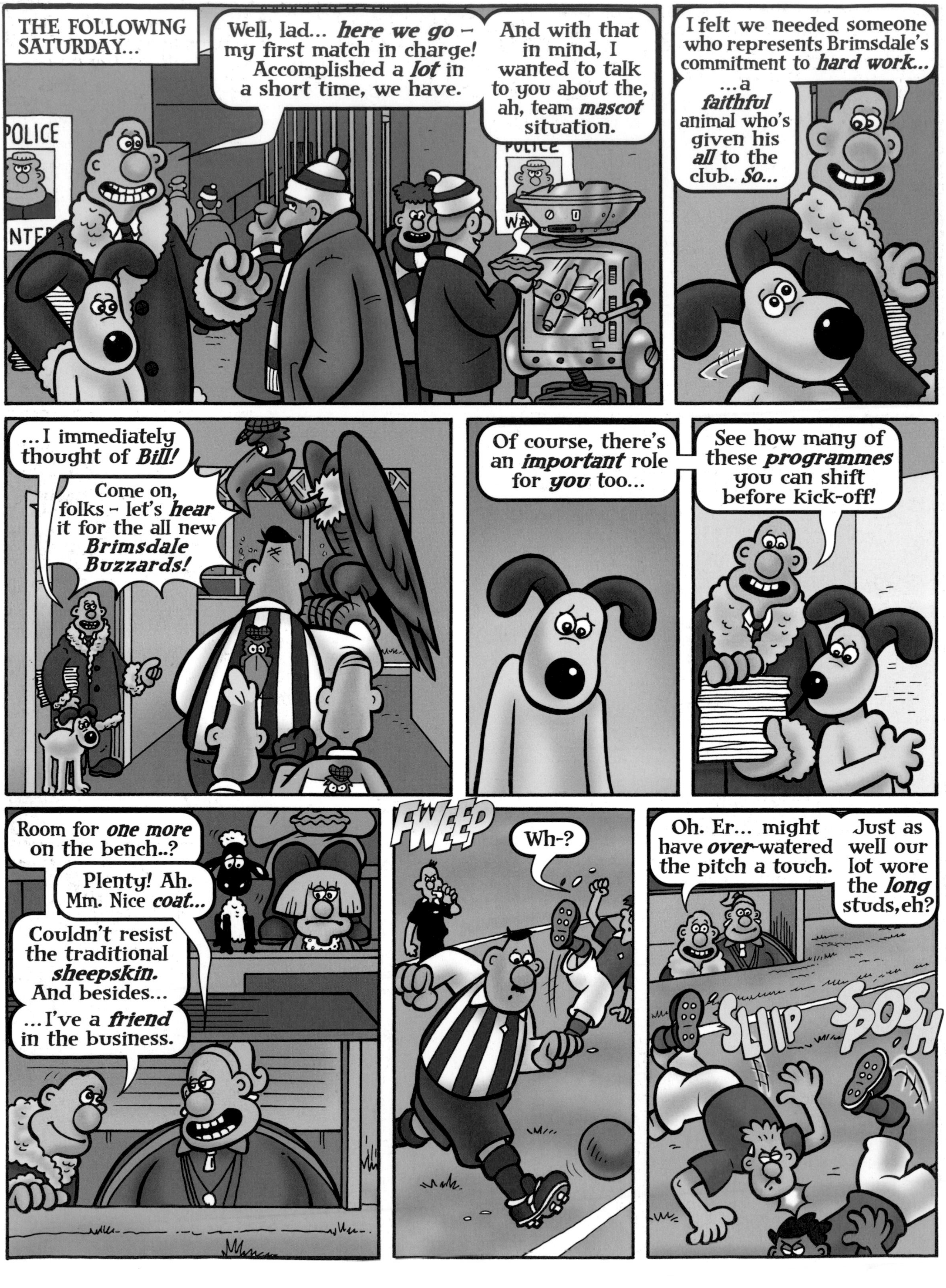
THE FOLLOWING SATURDAY...
Well, lad... here we go – my first match in charge! Accomplished a lot in a short time, we have.
And with that in mind, I wanted to talk to you about the, ah, team mascot situation.
I felt we needed someone who represents Brimsdale's commitment to hard work...
...a faithful animal who's given his all to the club. So...
...I immediately thought of Bill!
Come on, folks – let's hear it for the all new Brimsdale Buzzards!
Of course, there's an important role for you too...
See how many of these programmes you can shift before kick-off!
Room for one more on the bench..?
Plenty! Ah. Mm. Nice coat...
Couldn't resist the traditional sheepskin. And besides...
...I've a friend in the business.
FWEEP
Wh-?
Oh. Er... might have over-watered the pitch a touch.
Just as well our lot wore the long studs, eh?
SLIIP
SPOSH

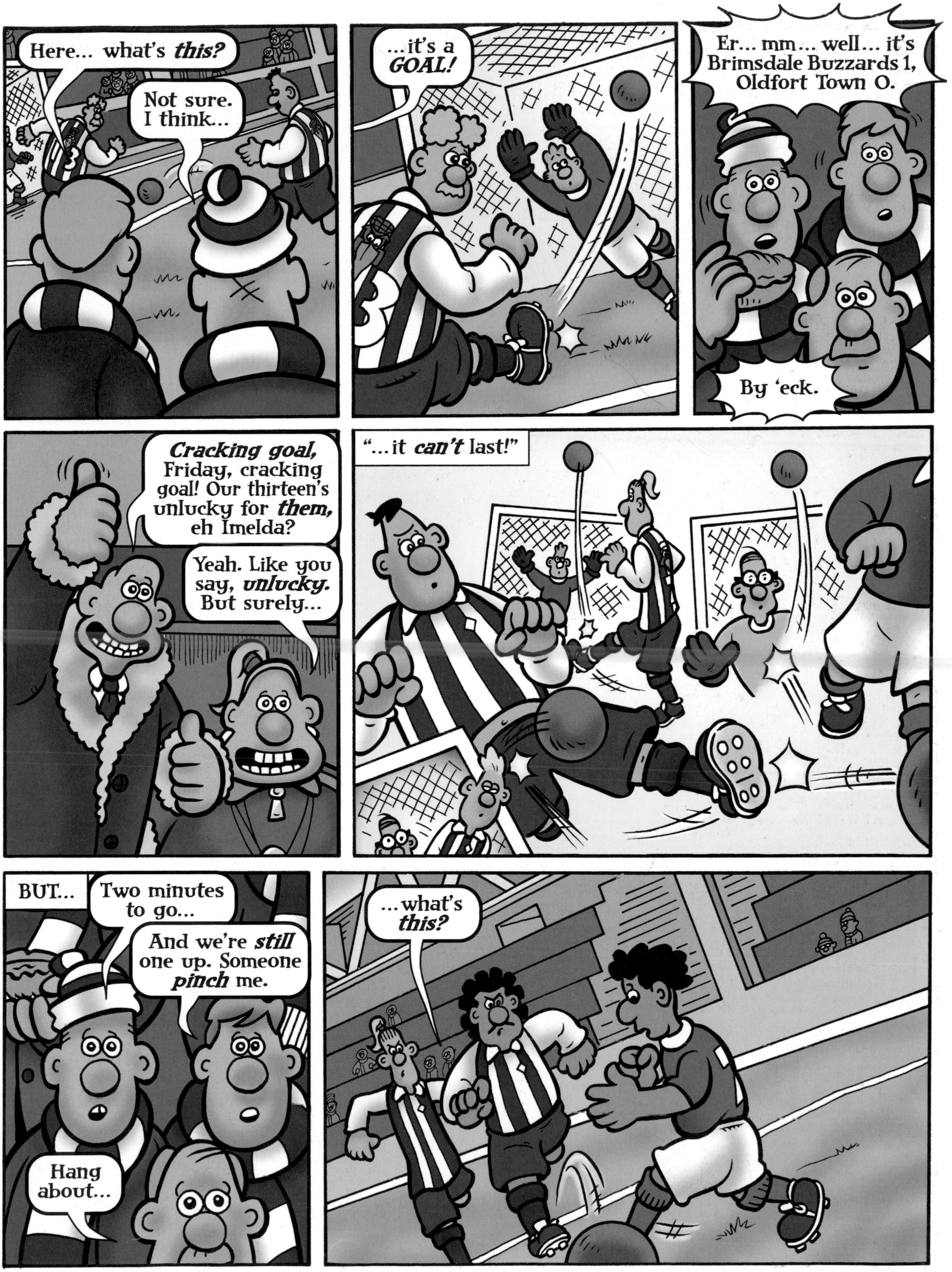
Here... what's *this?*
Not sure. I think...
...it's a *GOAL!*
Er... mm... well... it's Brimsdale Buzzards 1, Oldfort Town 0.
By 'eck.
Cracking goal, Friday, cracking goal! Our thirteen's unlucky for *them,* eh Imelda?
Yeah. Like you say, *unlucky.* But surely...
"...it *can't* last!"
BUT...
Two minutes to go...
And we're *still* one up. Someone *pinch* me.
Hang about...
...what's *this?*

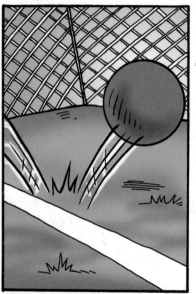

FWEEP

Yes! 2-0! The *beautiful game* returns to Brimsdale!

...unbelievable...

SHORTLY...

How about *that?* A *win*...

Turning point for Brimsdale, I reckon.

Ah. Don't count your chickens just yet. This lot...

EH-*OOOFF!*

WANTED

CLUNNG!

WANTED

...y'never know *what* to expect *next!*

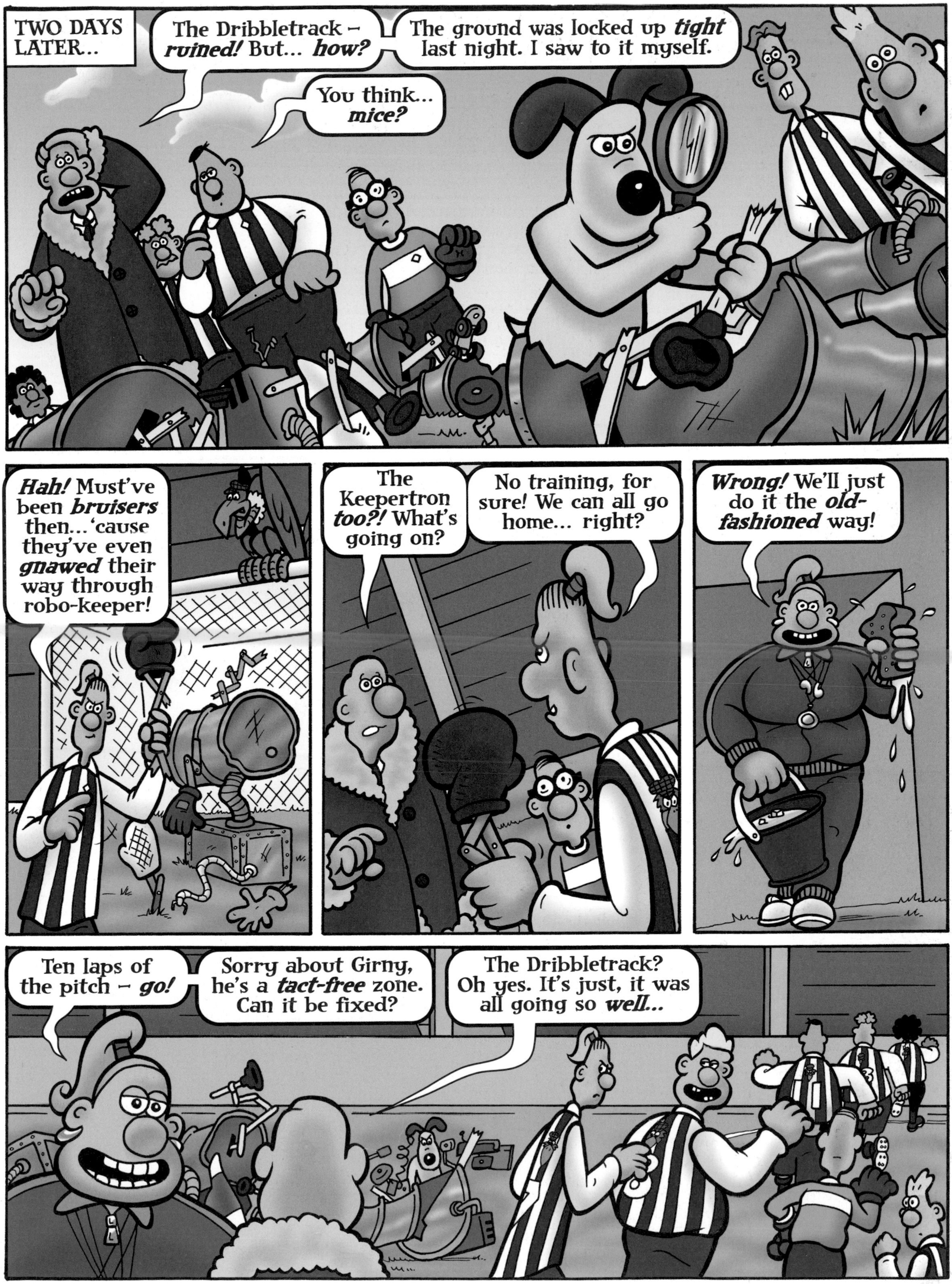
TWO DAYS LATER...
The Dribbletrack – *ruined!* But... *how?*
The ground was locked up *tight* last night. I saw to it myself.
You think... *mice?*
Hah! Must've been *bruisers* then...'cause they've even *gnawed* their way through robo-keeper!
The Keepertron *too?!* What's going on?
No training, for sure! We can all go home... right?
Wrong! We'll just do it the *old-fashioned* way!
Ten laps of the pitch – *go!*
Sorry about Girny, he's a *tact-free* zone. Can it be fixed?
The Dribbletrack? Oh yes. It's just, it was all going so *well...*

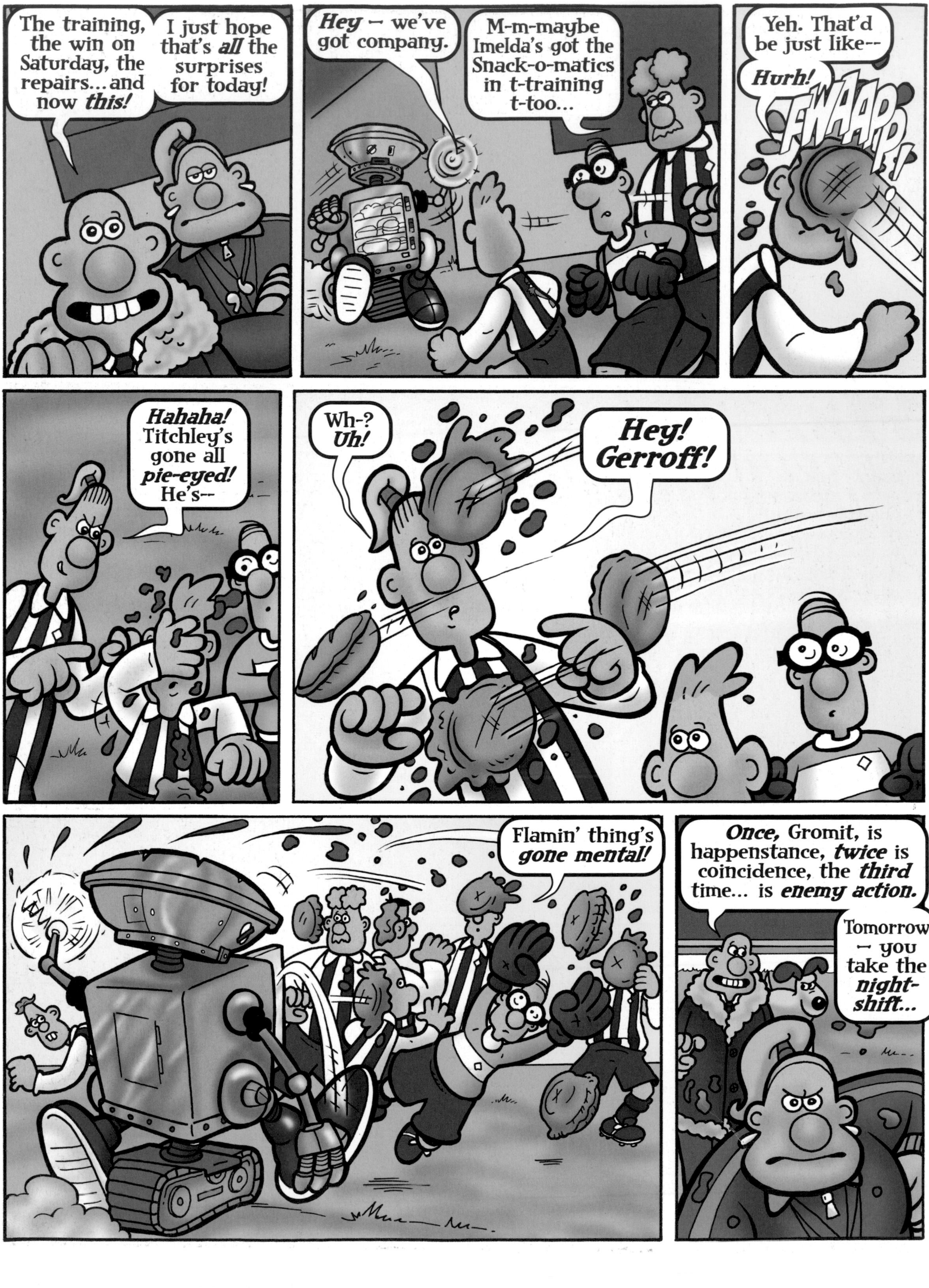

The training, the win on Saturday, the repairs... and now *this!*
I just hope that's *all* the surprises for today!
Hey — we've got company.
M-m-maybe Imelda's got the Snack-o-matics in t-training t-too...
Yeh. That'd be just like--
Hurh!
FWAAPP!
Hahaha! Titchley's gone all *pie-eyed!* He's--
Wh-? *Uh!*
Hey! Gerroff!
Flamin' thing's *gone mental!*
Once, Gromit, is happenstance, *twice* is coincidence, the *third* time... is *enemy action.*
Tomorrow — you take the *night-shift...*

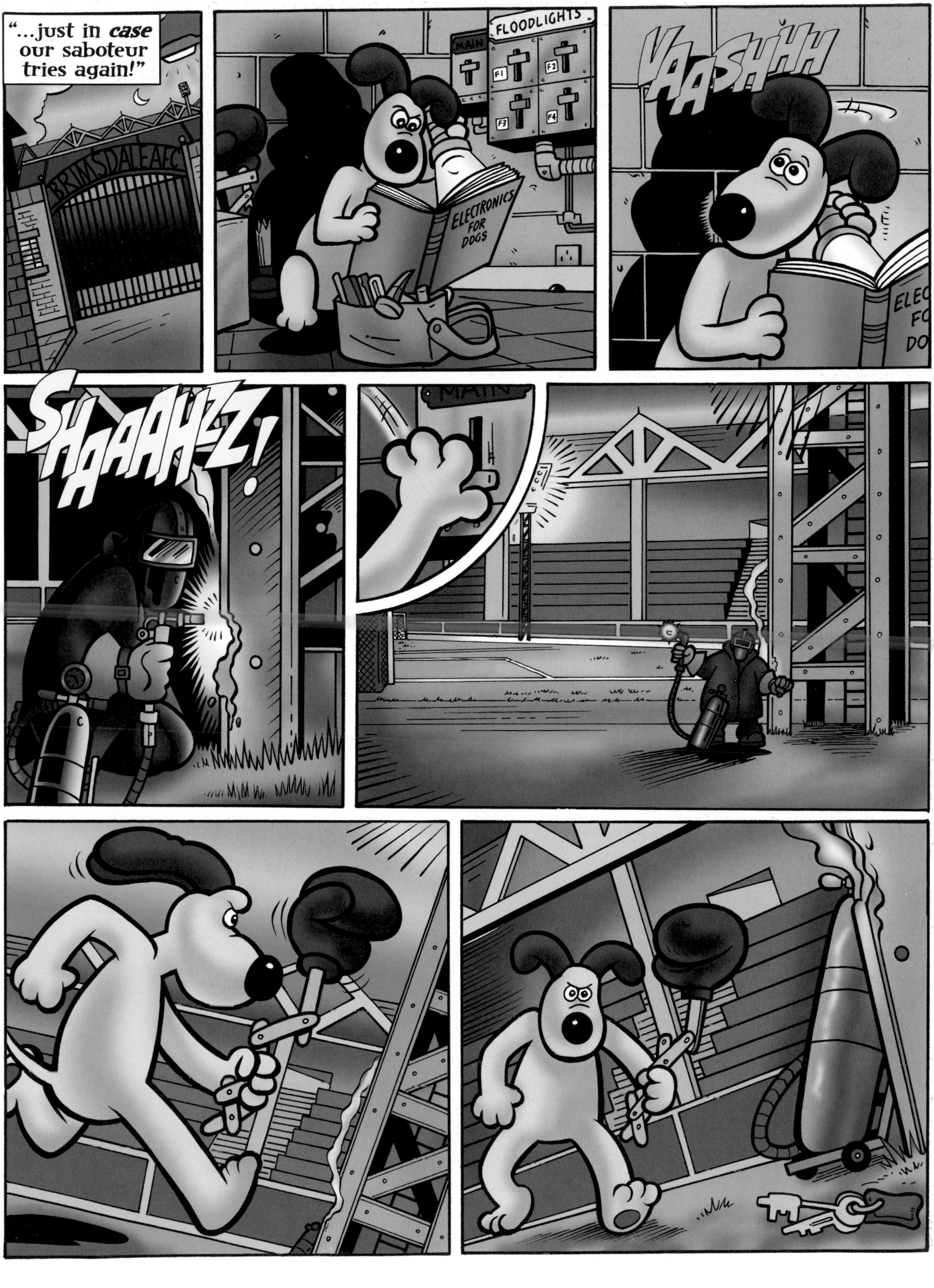
"...just in *case* our saboteur tries again!"
BRIMSDALE F.C.
MAIN
FLOODLIGHTS
F1
F2
F3
F4
ELECTRONICS FOR DOGS
VAASHHH
SHAAAHZZ!
MAIN

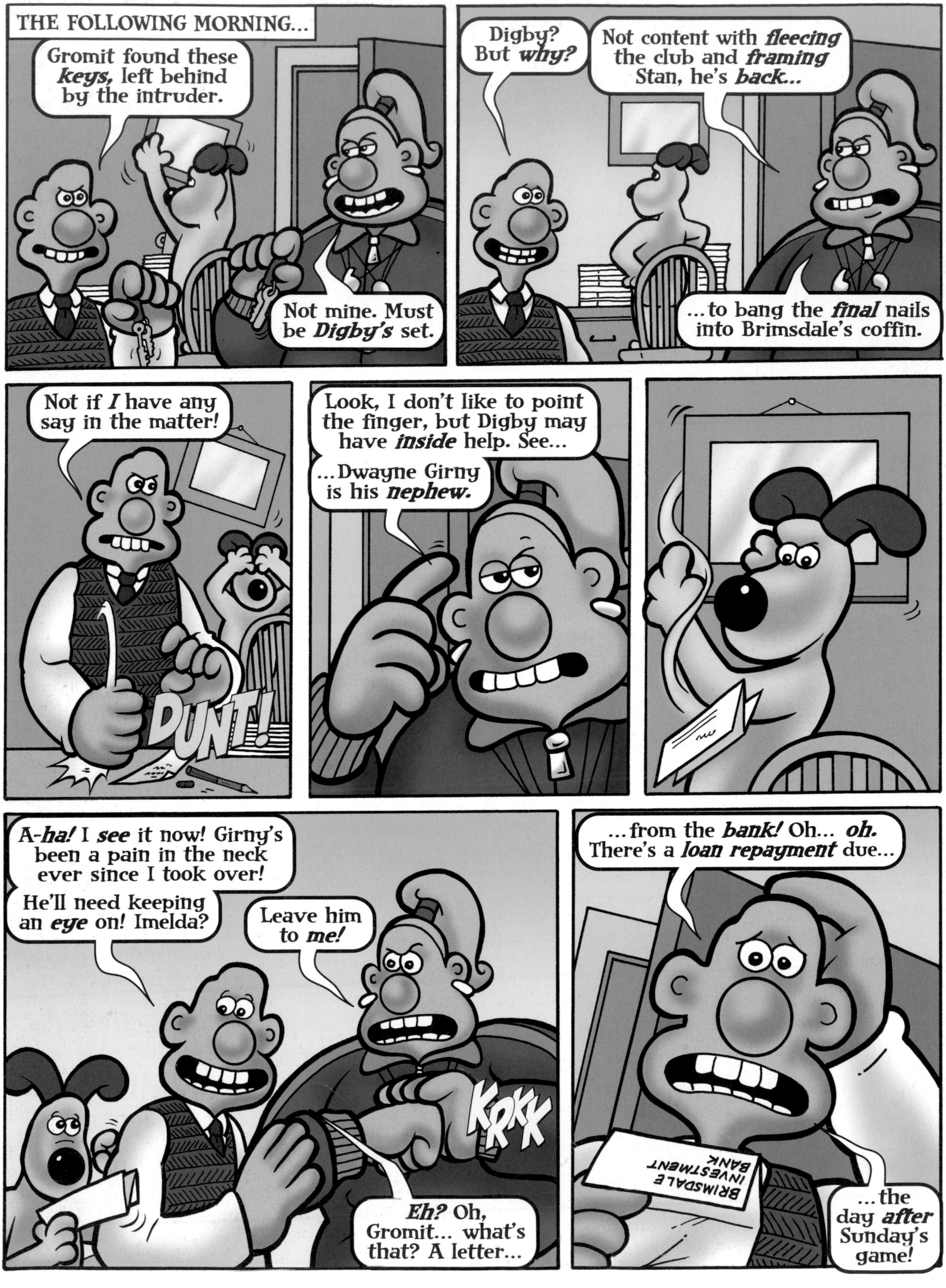
THE FOLLOWING MORNING...
Gromit found these *keys,* left behind by the intruder.
Not mine. Must be *Digby's* set.
Digby? But *why?*
Not content with *fleecing* the club and *framing* Stan, he's *back...*
...to bang the *final* nails into Brimsdale's coffin.
Not if *I* have any say in the matter!
DUNT!
Look, I don't like to point the finger, but Digby may have *inside* help. See...
...Dwayne Girny is his *nephew.*
A-*ha!* I *see* it now! Girny's been a pain in the neck ever since I took over!
He'll need keeping an *eye* on! Imelda?
Leave him to *me!*
KRKK
Eh? Oh, Gromit... what's that? A letter...
...from the *bank!* Oh... *oh.* There's a *loan repayment* due...
BRIMSDALE INVESTMENT BANK
...the day *after* Sunday's game!

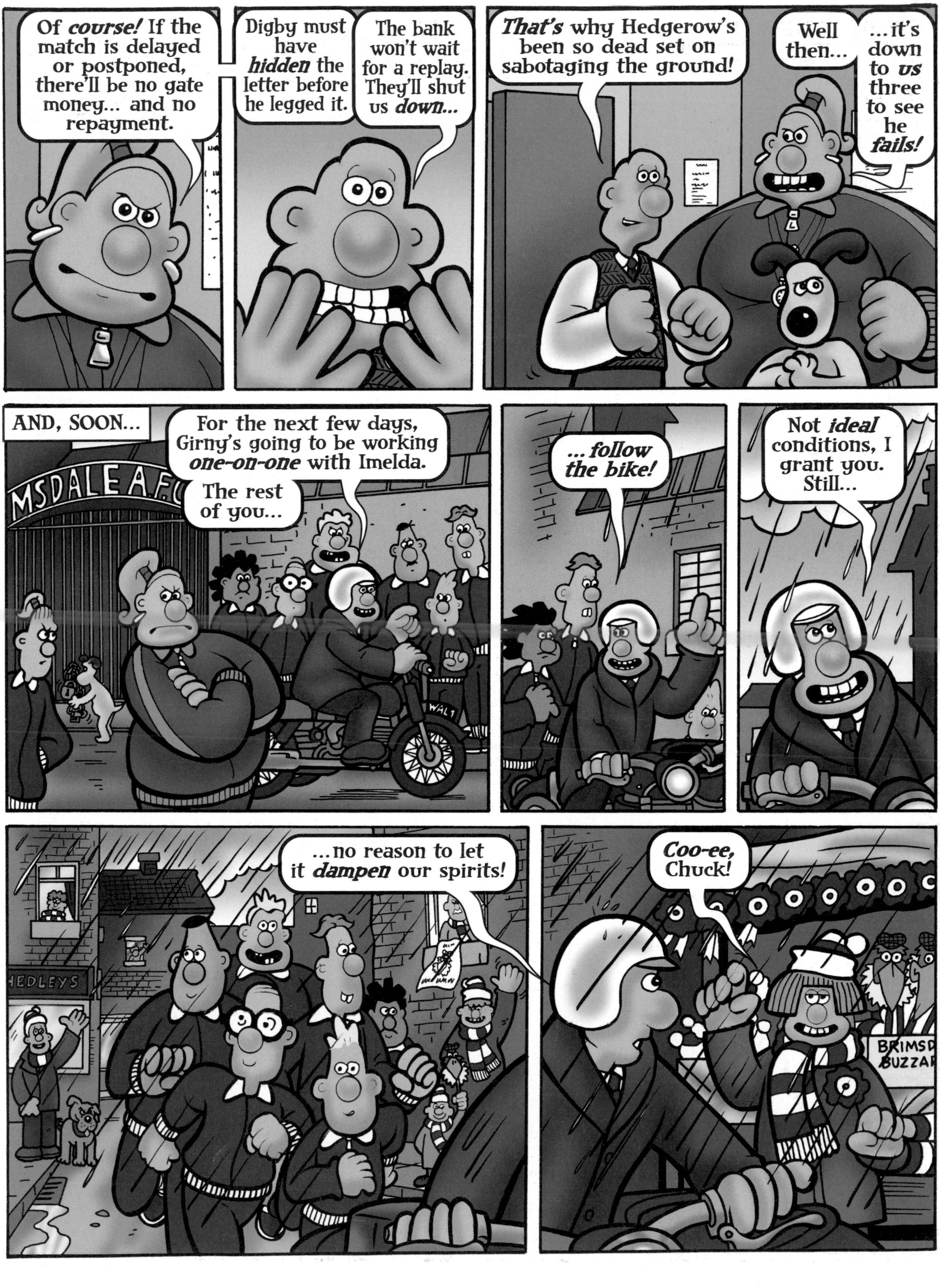
Of *course!* If the match is delayed or postponed, there'll be no gate money... and no repayment.
Digby must have *hidden* the letter before he legged it.
The bank won't wait for a replay. They'll shut us *down...*
That's why Hedgerow's been so dead set on sabotaging the ground!
Well then...
...it's down to *us* three to see he *fails!*
AND, SOON...
MSDALE A.F.C
For the next few days, Girny's going to be working *one-on-one* with Imelda.
The rest of you...
WAL 1
...follow the bike!
Not *ideal* conditions, I grant you. Still...
...no reason to let it *dampen* our spirits!
HEDLEYS
Coo-ee, Chuck!
BRIMSD
BUZZAR

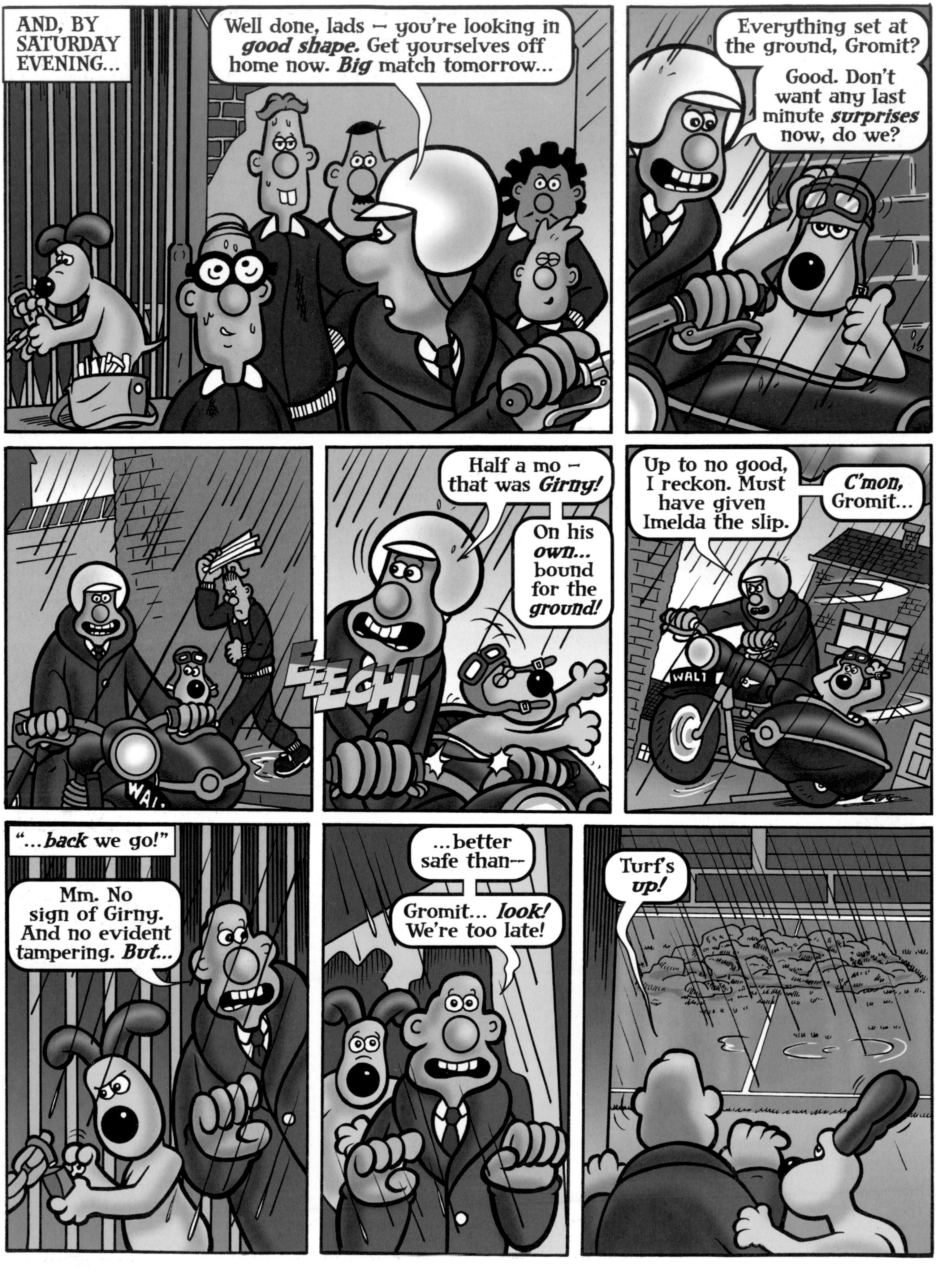

AND, BY SATURDAY EVENING...
Well done, lads – you're looking in *good shape.* Get yourselves off home now. *Big* match tomorrow...
Everything set at the ground, Gromit?
Good. Don't want any last minute *surprises* now, do we?
Half a mo – that was *Girny!*
On his *own...* bound for the *ground!*
EEECH!
Up to no good, I reckon. Must have given Imelda the slip.
C'mon, Gromit...
"...*back* we go!"
Mm. No sign of Girny. And no evident tampering. *But...*
...better safe than--
Gromit... *look!* We're too late!
Turf's *up!*

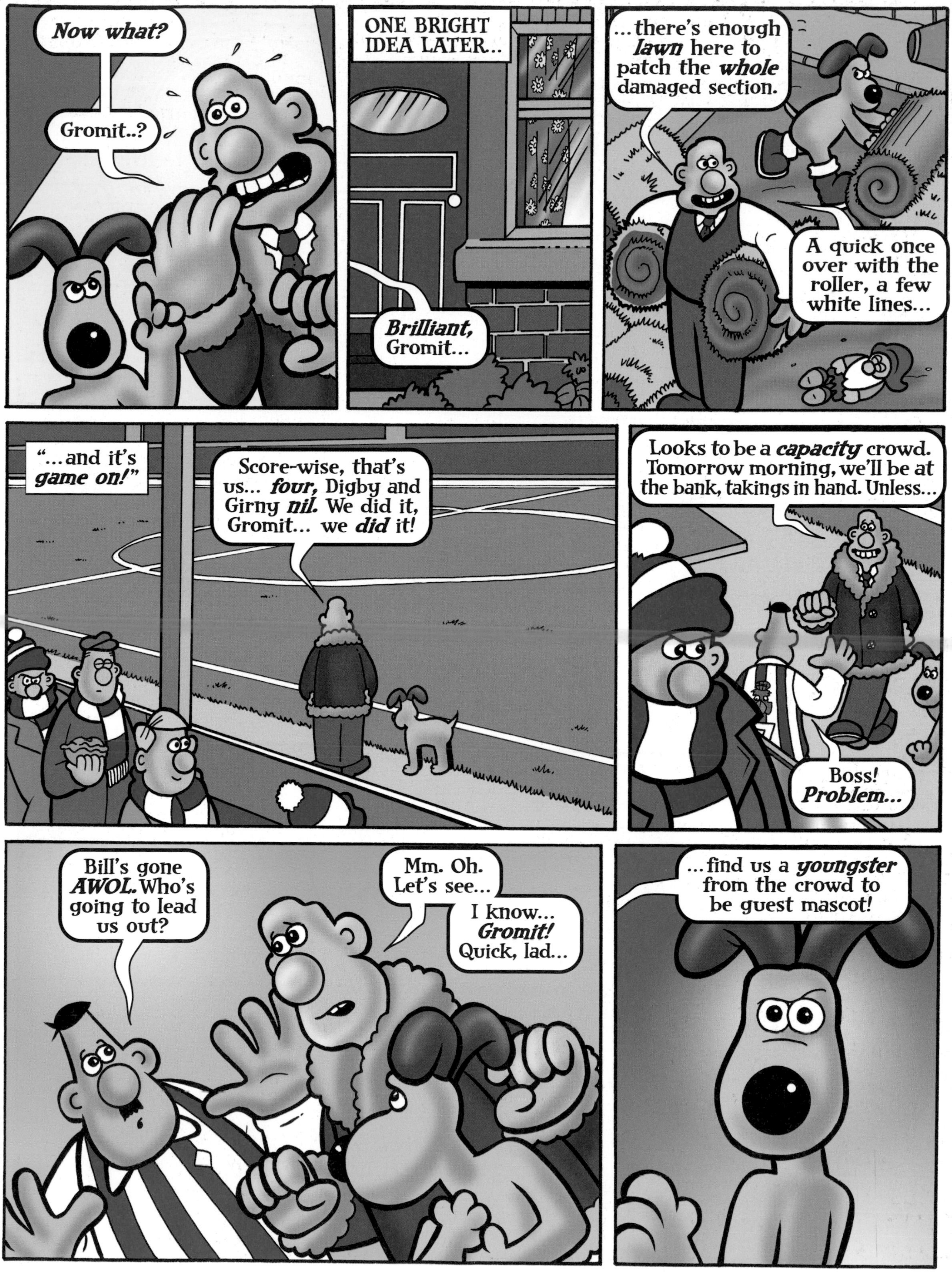

Now what?
Gromit..?
ONE BRIGHT IDEA LATER...
Brilliant, Gromit...
...there's enough lawn here to patch the whole damaged section.
A quick once over with the roller, a few white lines...
"...and it's game on!"
Score-wise, that's us... four, Digby and Girny nil. We did it, Gromit... we did it!
Looks to be a capacity crowd. Tomorrow morning, we'll be at the bank, takings in hand. Unless...
Boss! Problem...
Bill's gone AWOL. Who's going to lead us out?
Mm. Oh. Let's see...
I know... Gromit! Quick, lad...
...find us a youngster from the crowd to be guest mascot!

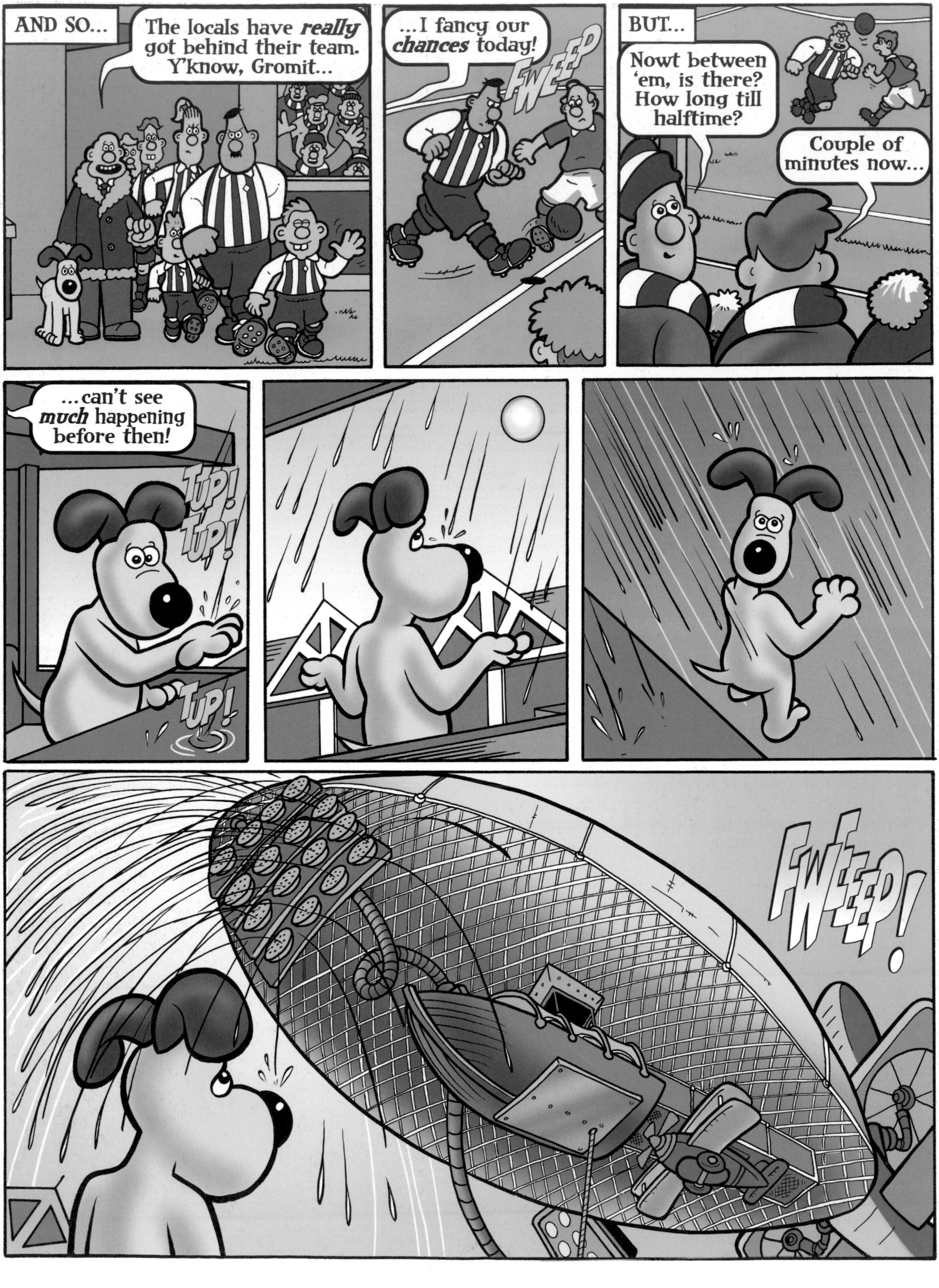
AND SO...
The locals have *really* got behind their team. Y'know, Gromit...
...I fancy our *chances* today!
FWEEP
BUT...
Nowt between 'em, is there? How long till halftime?
Couple of minutes now...
...can't see *much* happening before then!
TUP! TUP!
TUP!
FWEEEP!

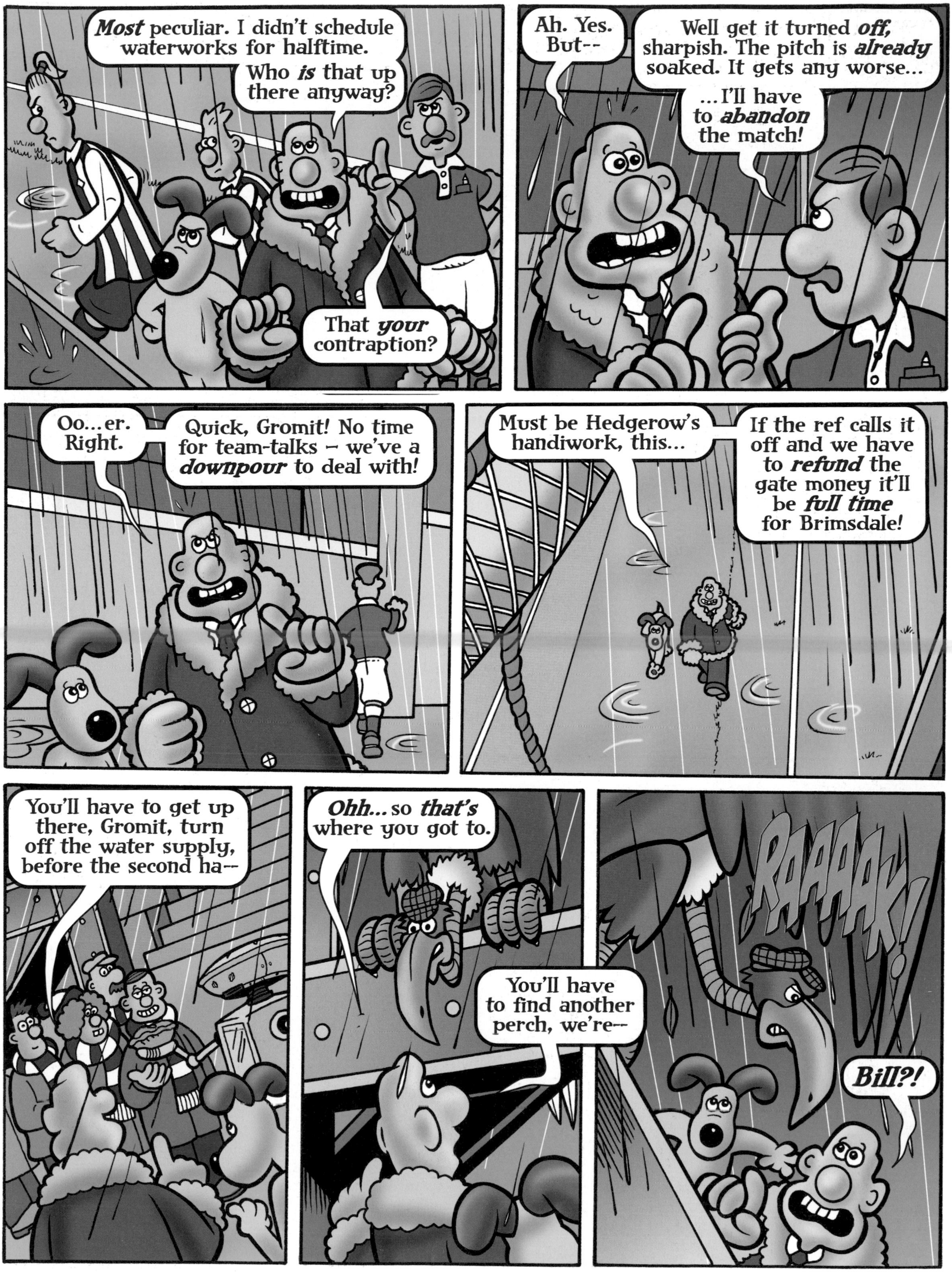
Most peculiar. I didn't schedule waterworks for halftime.
Who is that up there anyway?
That your contraption?
Ah. Yes. But--
Well get it turned off, sharpish. The pitch is already soaked. It gets any worse...
...I'll have to abandon the match!
Oo...er. Right.
Quick, Gromit! No time for team-talks – we've a downpour to deal with!
Must be Hedgerow's handiwork, this...
If the ref calls it off and we have to refund the gate money it'll be full time for Brimsdale!
You'll have to get up there, Gromit, turn off the water supply, before the second ha--
Ohh... so that's where you got to.
You'll have to find another perch, we're--
RAAAAK!
Bill?!

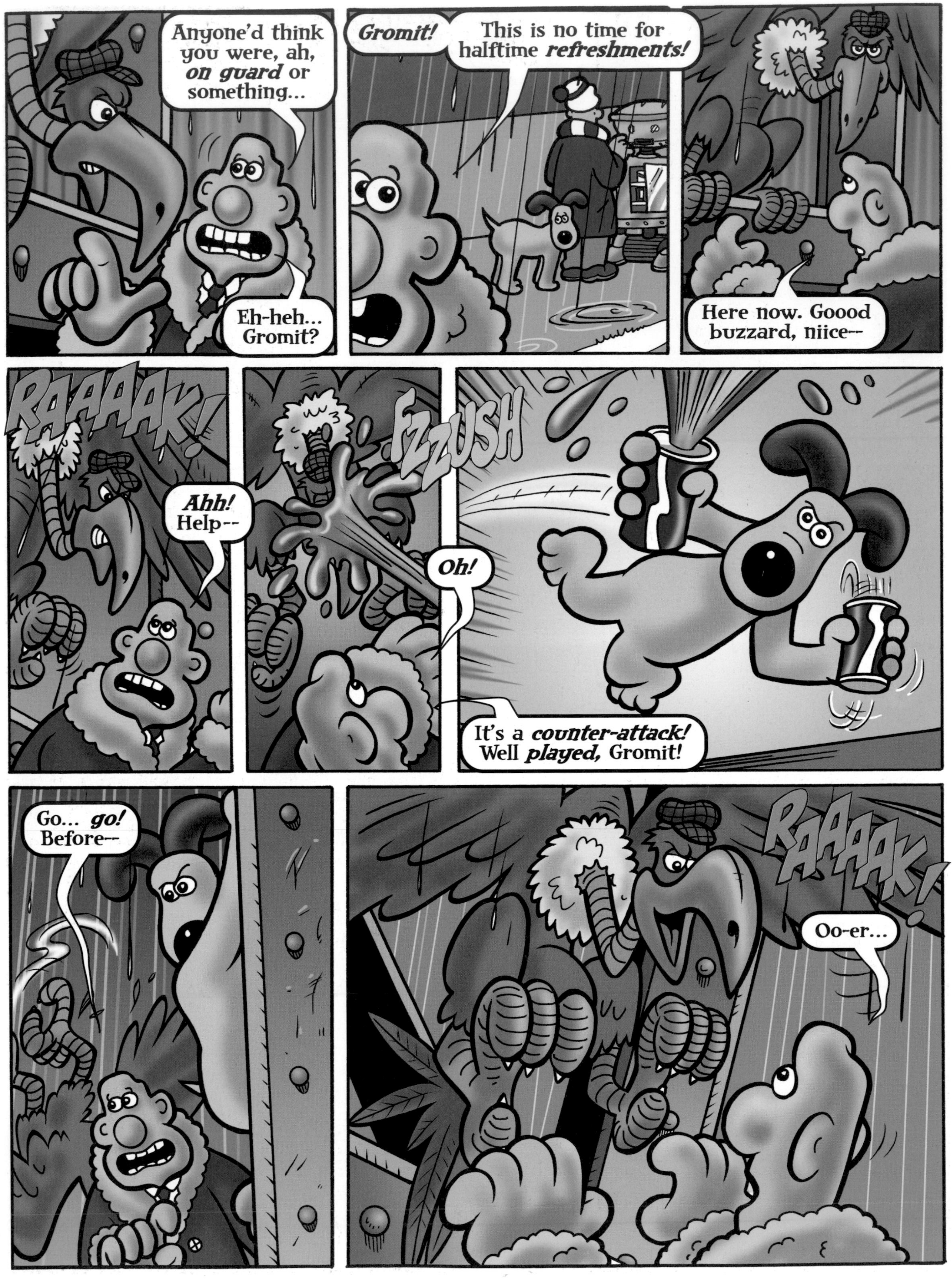
Anyone'd think you were, ah, *on guard* or something...
Eh-heh... Gromit?
Gromit!
This is no time for halftime *refreshments!*
Here now. Goood buzzard, niice--
RAAAAK!
Ahh! Help--
FZZUSH
Oh!
It's a *counter-attack!* Well *played,* Gromit!
Go... *go!* Before--
RAAAAK!
Oo-er...

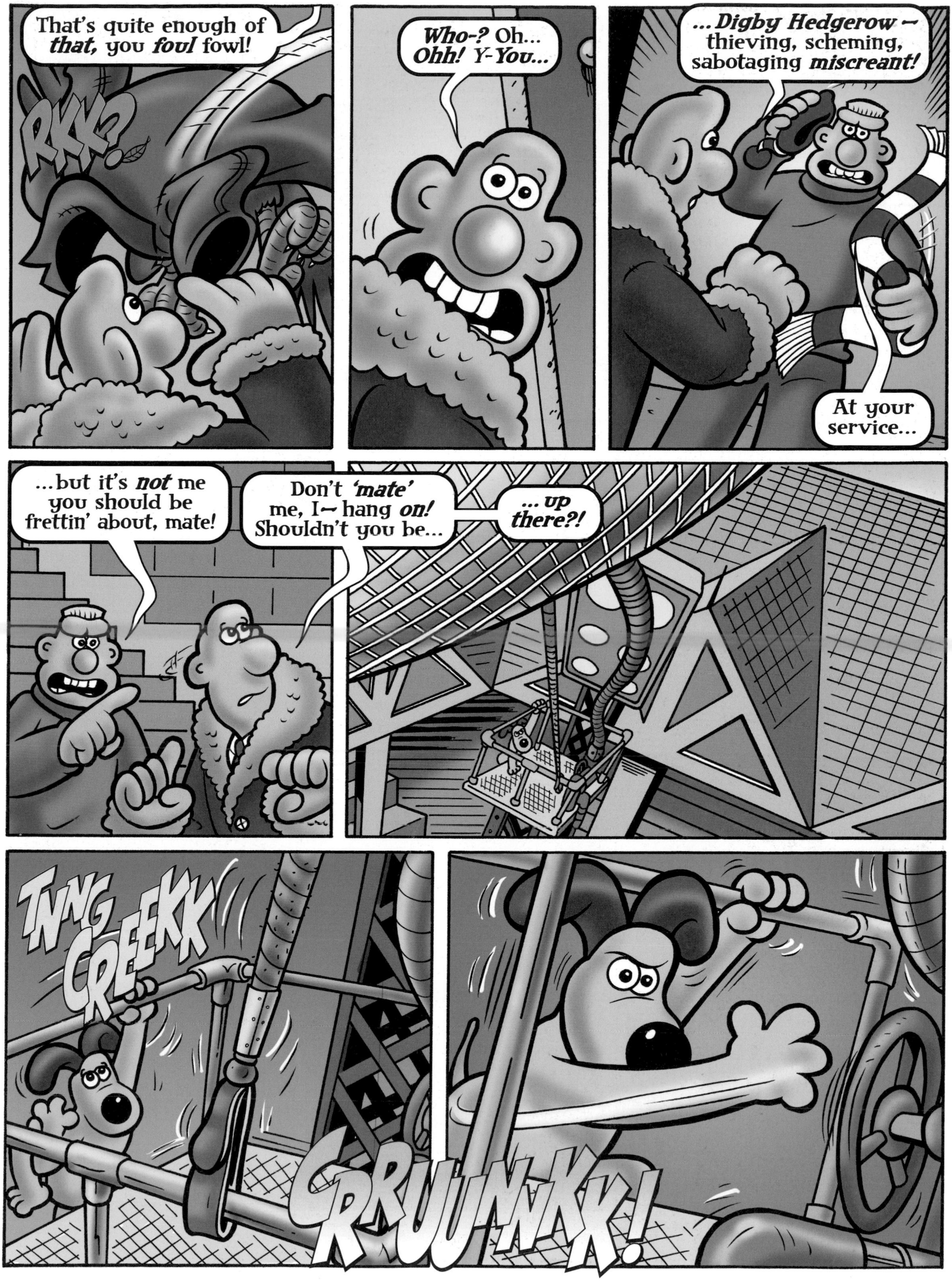
That's quite enough of *that,* you *foul* fowl!
RKK?
Who-? Oh... *Ohh!* Y-*You...*
...Digby Hedgerow — thieving, scheming, sabotaging *miscreant!*
At your service...
...but it's *not* me you should be frettin' about, mate!
Don't *'mate'* me, I— hang *on!* Shouldn't you be...
...up there?!
TNNG
CREEKK
CRUUNKK!

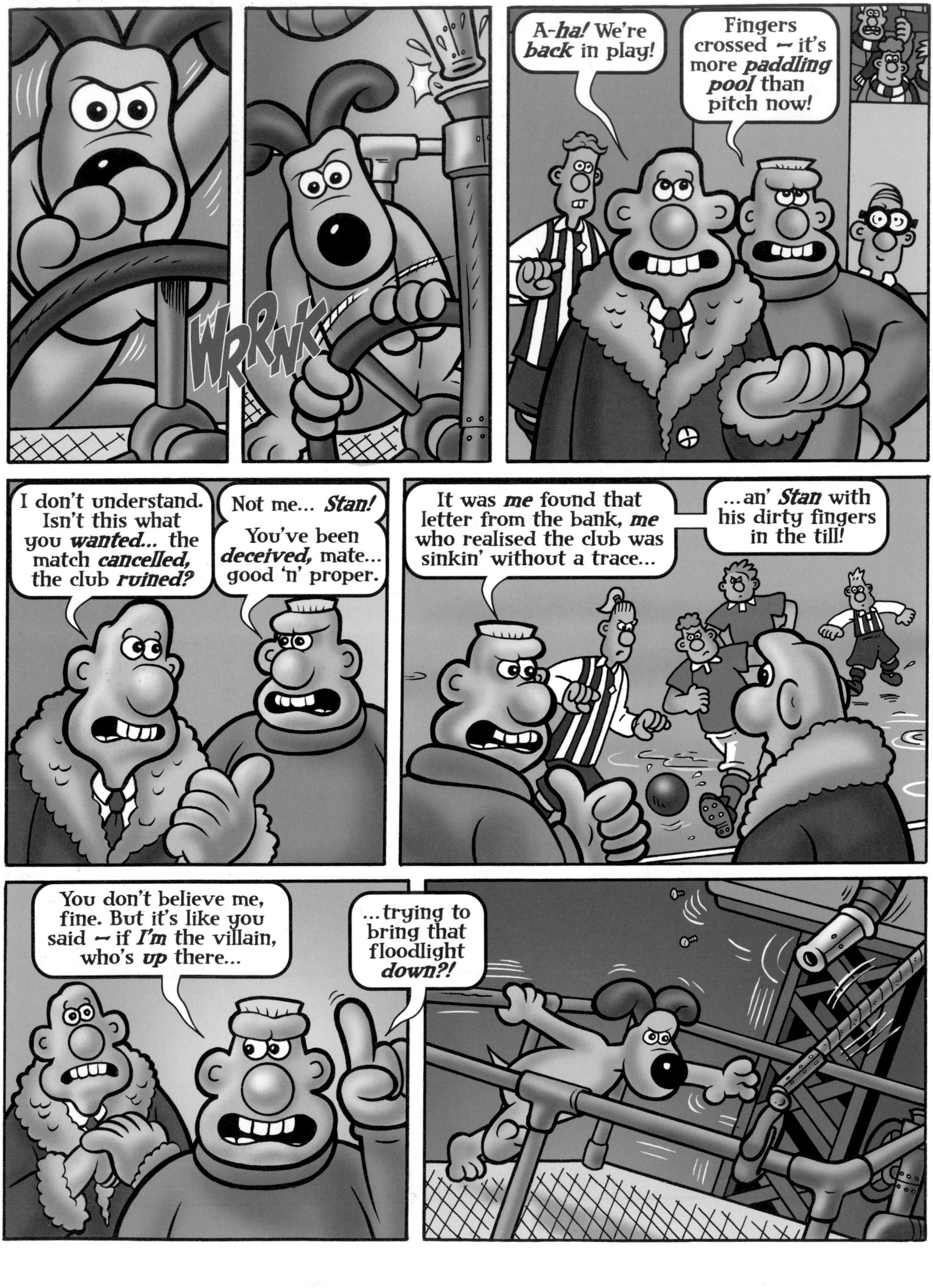
WRRNK
A-ha! We're back in play!
Fingers crossed – it's more paddling pool than pitch now!
I don't understand. Isn't this what you wanted... the match cancelled, the club ruined?
Not me... Stan!
You've been deceived, mate... good 'n' proper.
It was me found that letter from the bank, me who realised the club was sinkin' without a trace...
...an' Stan with his dirty fingers in the till!
You don't believe me, fine. But it's like you said – if I'm the villain, who's up there...
...trying to bring that floodlight down?!

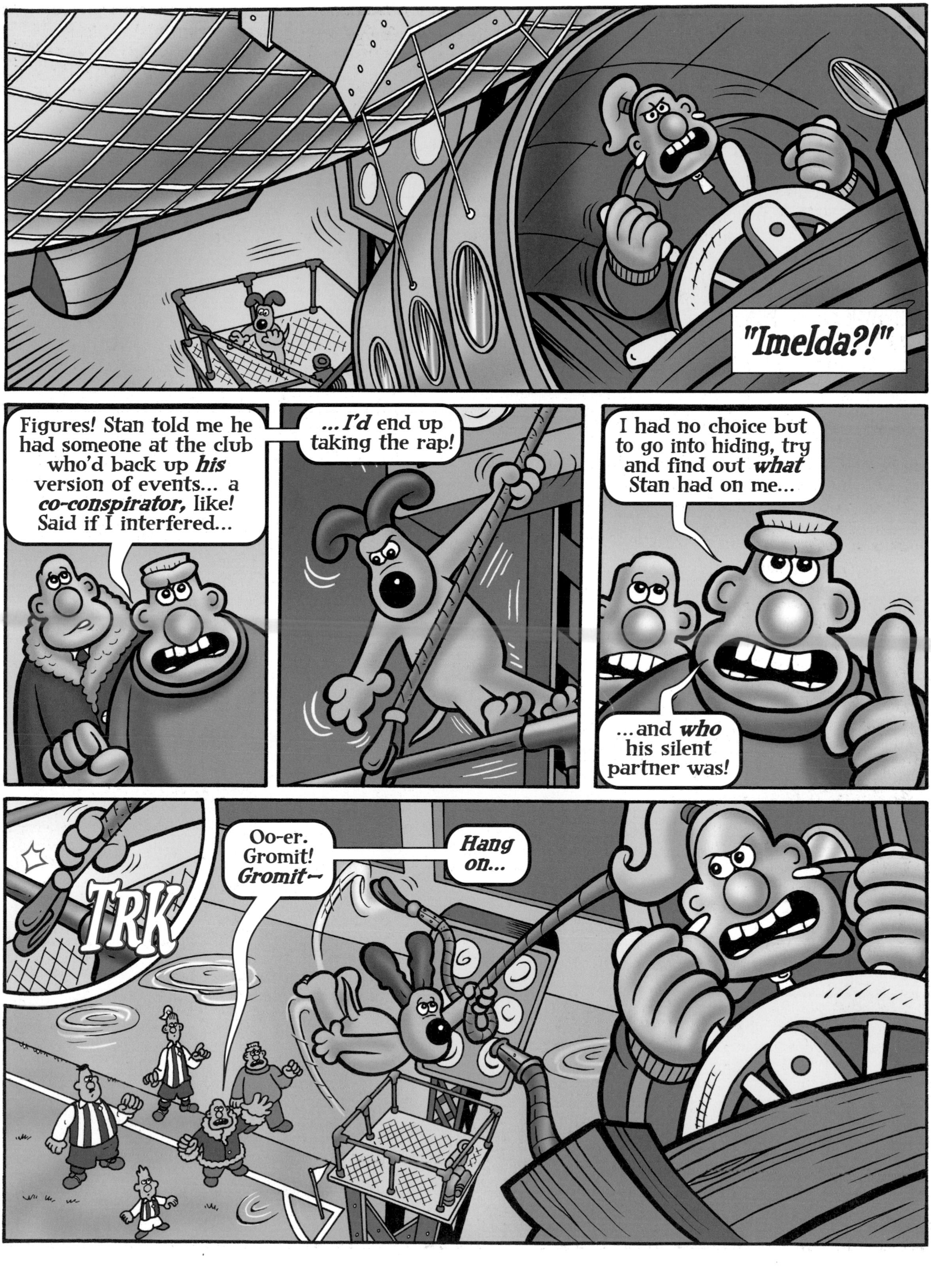
"Imelda?!"
Figures! Stan told me he had someone at the club who'd back up *his* version of events... a *co-conspirator,* like! Said if I interfered...
...*I'd* end up taking the rap!
I had no choice but to go into hiding, try and find out *what* Stan had on me...
...and *who* his silent partner was!
TRK
Oo-er. Gromit! *Gromit*--
Hang on...

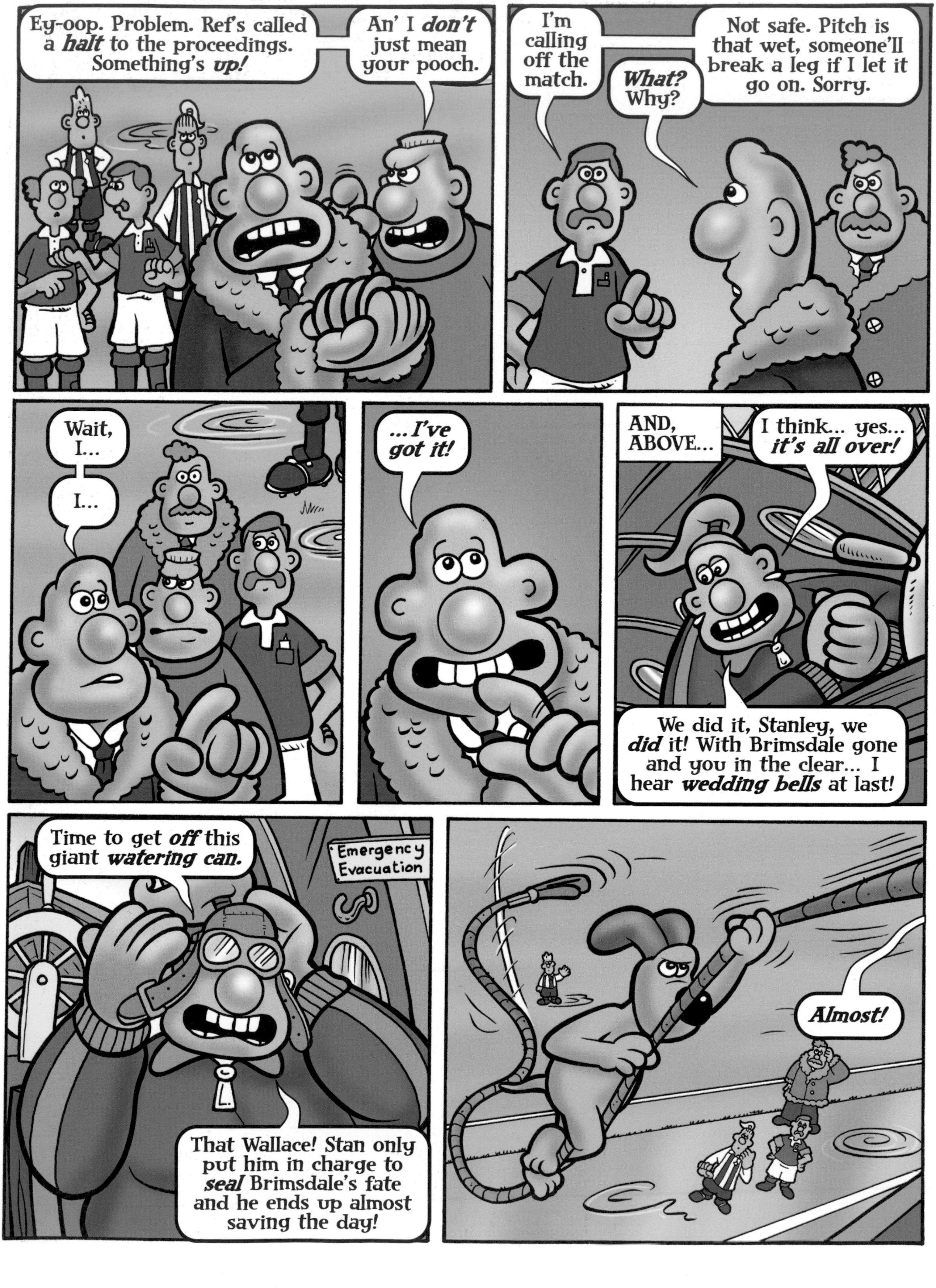

Ey-oop. Problem. Ref's called a *halt* to the proceedings. Something's *up!*
An' I *don't* just mean your pooch.
I'm calling off the match.
What? Why?
Not safe. Pitch is that wet, someone'll break a leg if I let it go on. Sorry.
Wait, I...
I...
...*I've got it!*
AND, ABOVE...
I think... yes... *it's all over!*
We did it, Stanley, we *did* it! With Brimsdale gone and you in the clear... I hear *wedding bells* at last!
Time to get *off* this giant *watering can.*
Emergency Evacuation
That Wallace! Stan only put him in charge to *seal* Brimsdale's fate and he ends up almost saving the day!
Almost!

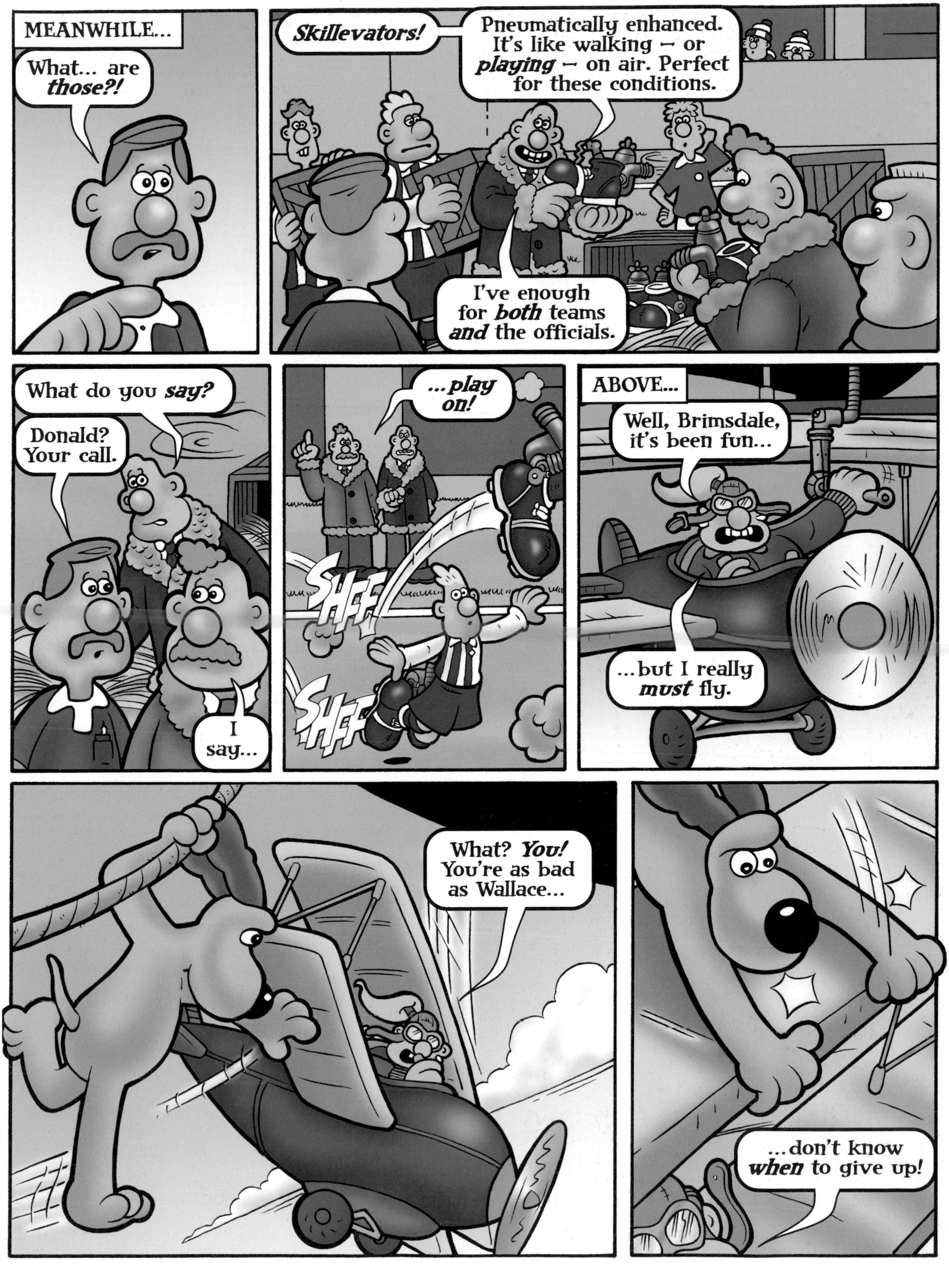
MEANWHILE...
What... are *those?!*
Skillevators!
Pneumatically enhanced. It's like walking – or *playing* – on air. Perfect for these conditions.
I've enough for *both* teams *and* the officials.
What do you *say?*
Donald? Your call.
I say...
...play on!
SHFF
SHFF
ABOVE...
Well, Brimsdale, it's been fun...
...but I really *must* fly.
What? *You!* You're as bad as Wallace...
...don't know *when* to give up!

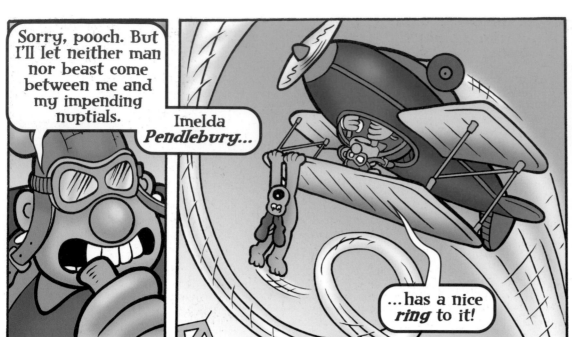

Sorry, pooch. But I'll let neither man nor beast come between me and my impending nuptials.

Imelda *Pendlebury*...

...has a nice *ring* to it!

We advise passengers to return to their seats and *fasten* safety belts...

...we're in for some *chop!*

BELOW...

Hh-*hh*. Called the *police*. They're on their way. How's it *goin'* up there?

Ah. Mm. Well...

"...Gromit's still on her *tail!*"

Oh for goodness *sake!*

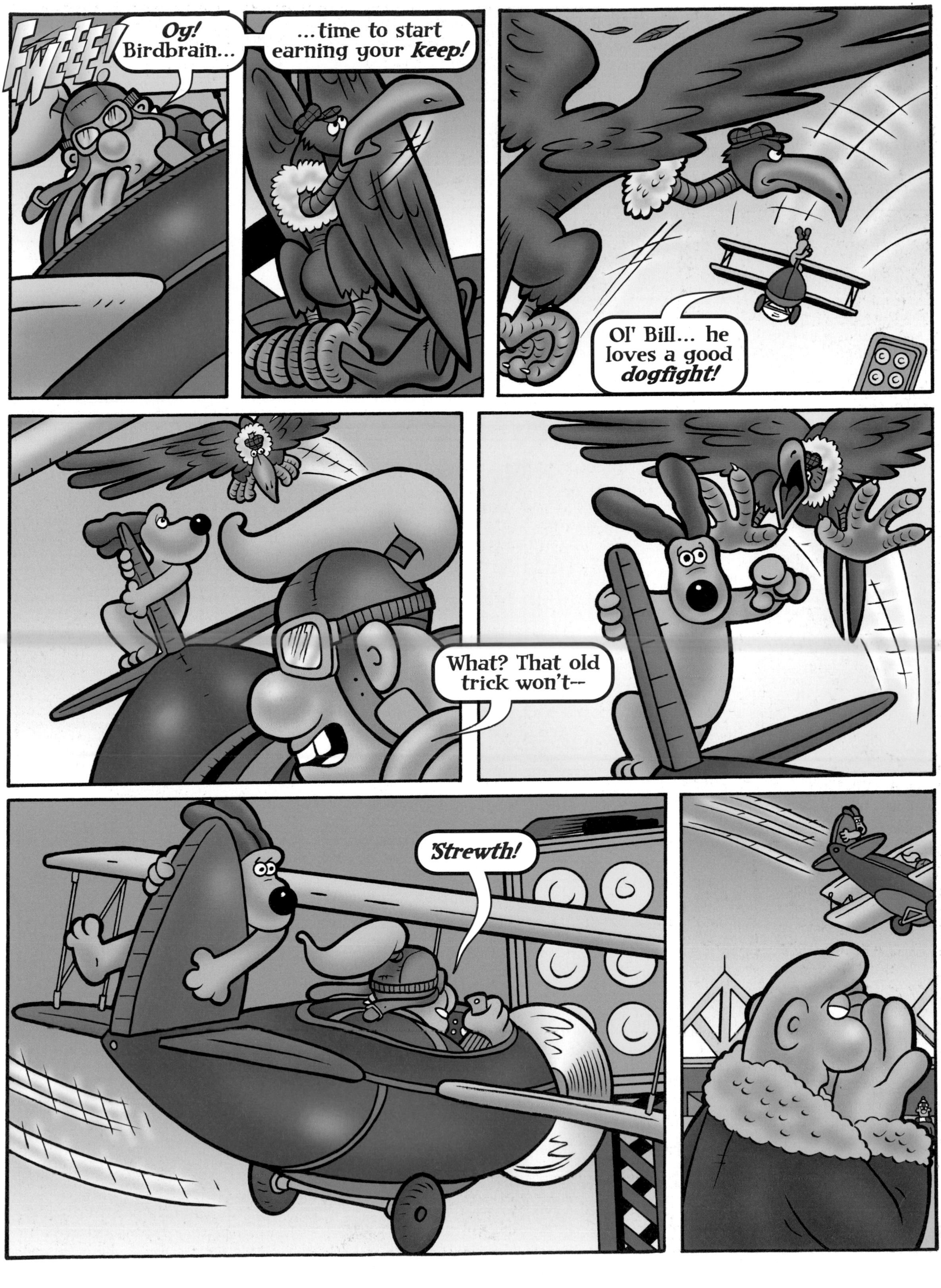
FWEEE!
Oy! Birdbrain...
...time to start earning your *keep!*
Ol' Bill... he loves a good *dogfight!*
What? That old trick won't--
'Strewth!

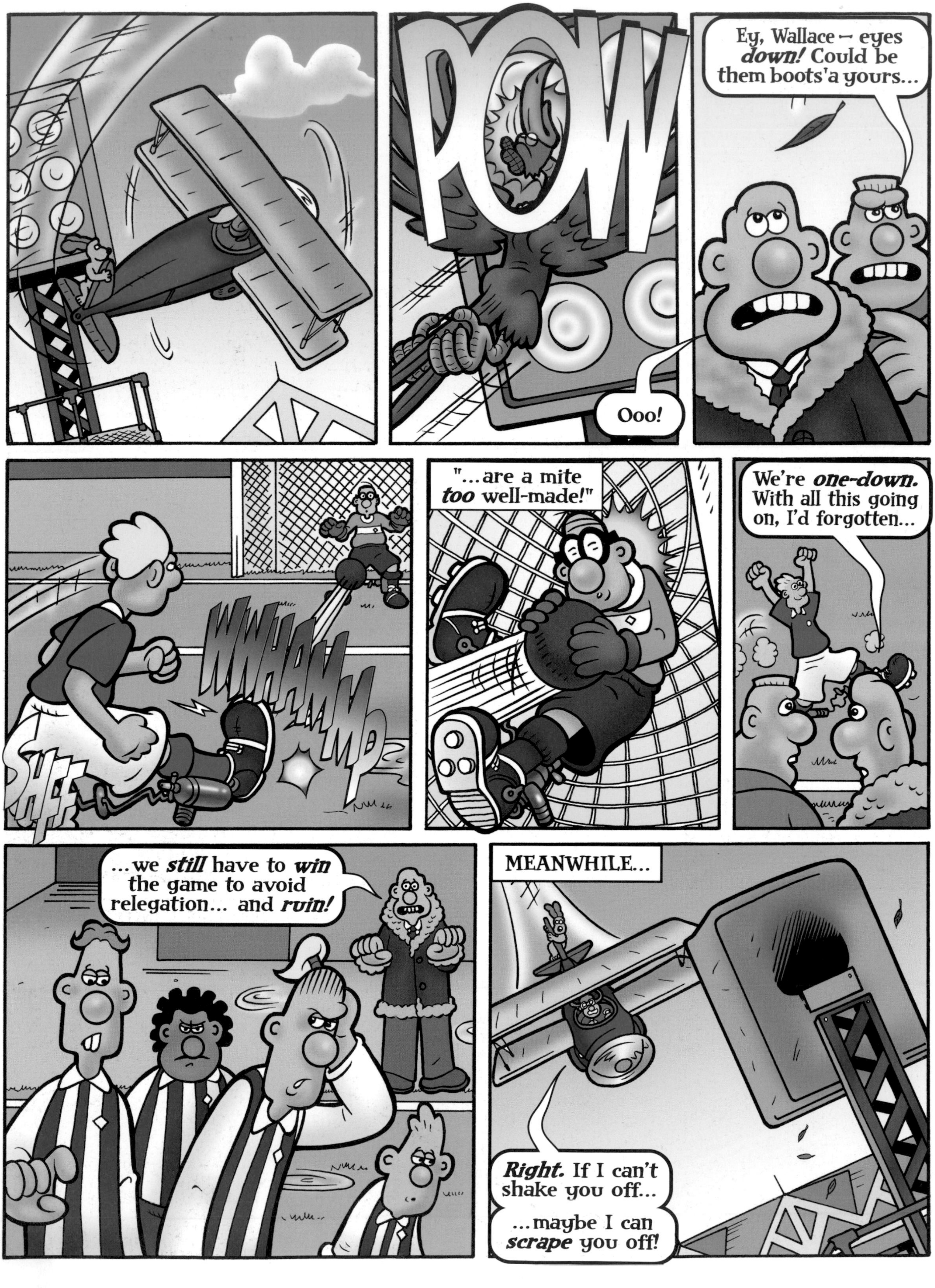
POW
Ey, Wallace – eyes down! Could be them boots'a yours...
Ooo!
WHAMMP
"...are a mite too well-made!"
We're one-down. With all this going on, I'd forgotten...
...we still have to win the game to avoid relegation... and ruin!
MEANWHILE...
Right. If I can't shake you off...
...maybe I can scrape you off!

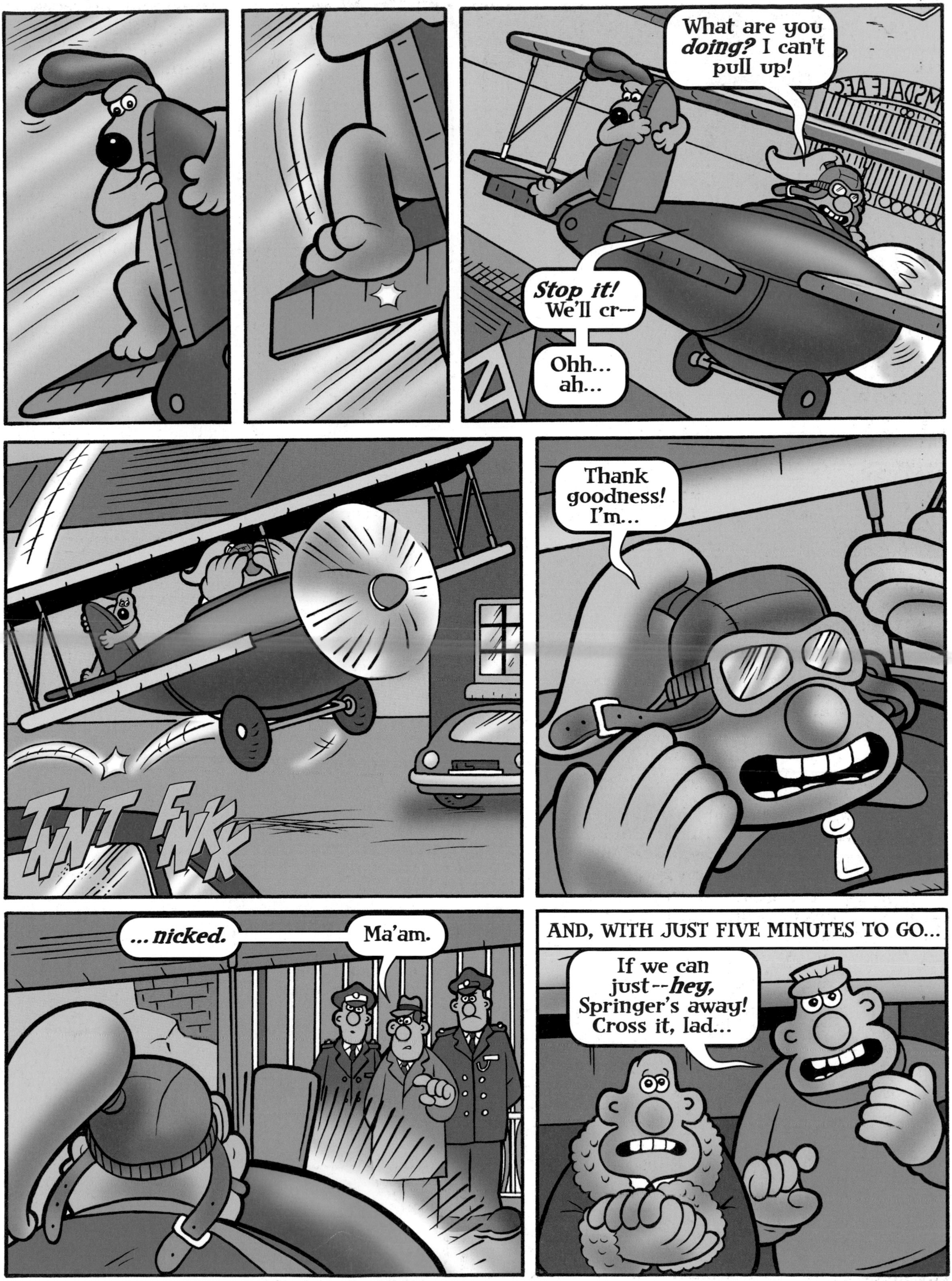
What are you doing? I can't pull up!
Stop it! We'll cr--
Ohh... ah...
Thank goodness! I'm...
...nicked.
Ma'am.
AND, WITH JUST FIVE MINUTES TO GO...
If we can just--hey, Springer's away! Cross it, lad...

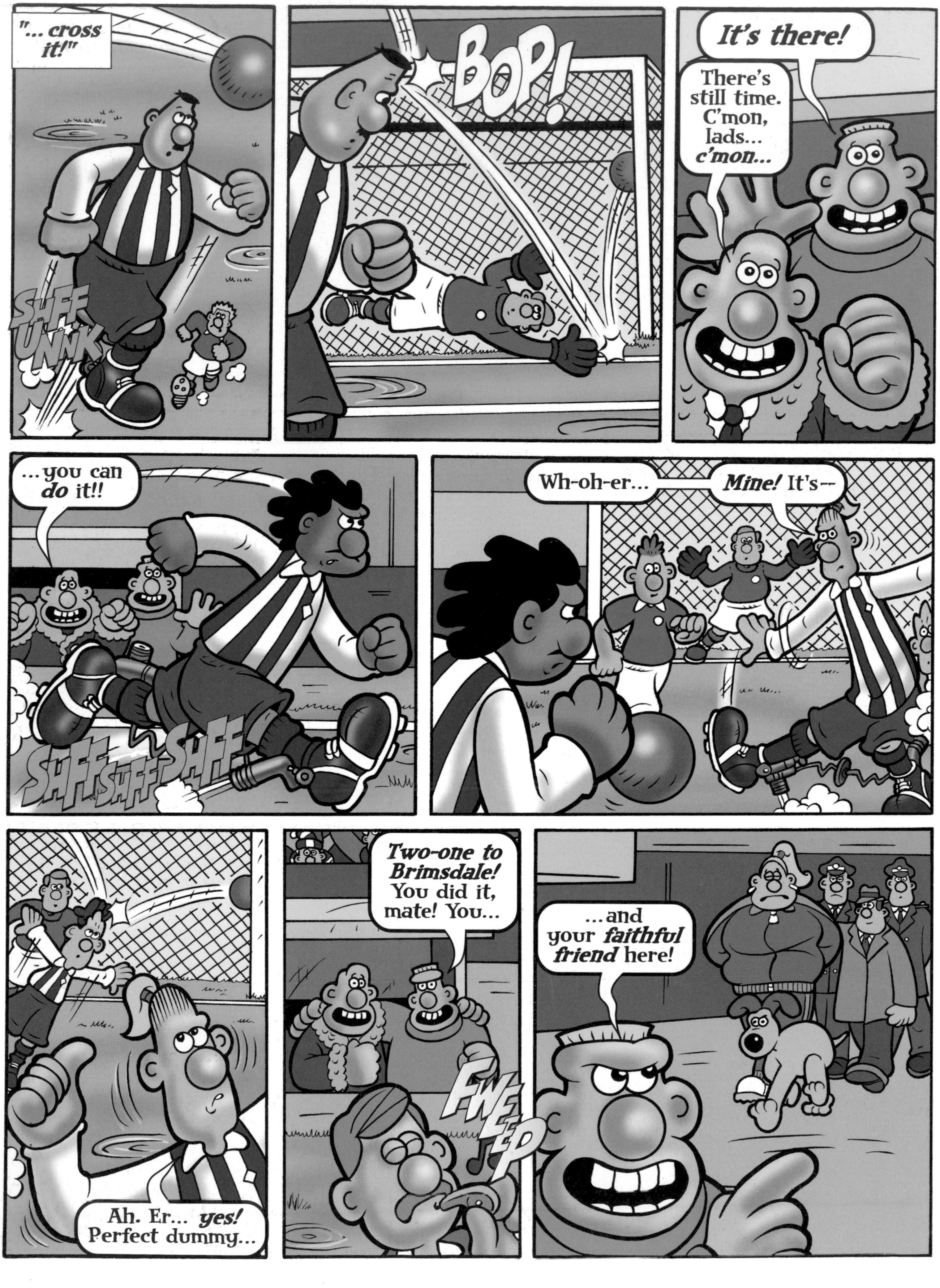

"... cross it!"
SHFF
UNNK
BOP!
It's there!
There's still time. C'mon, lads... c'mon...
...you can do it!!
SHFF SHFF SHFF
Wh-oh-er...
Mine! It's--
Ah. Er... yes! Perfect dummy...
Two-one to Brimsdale! You did it, mate! You...
FWEEP
...and your faithful friend here!

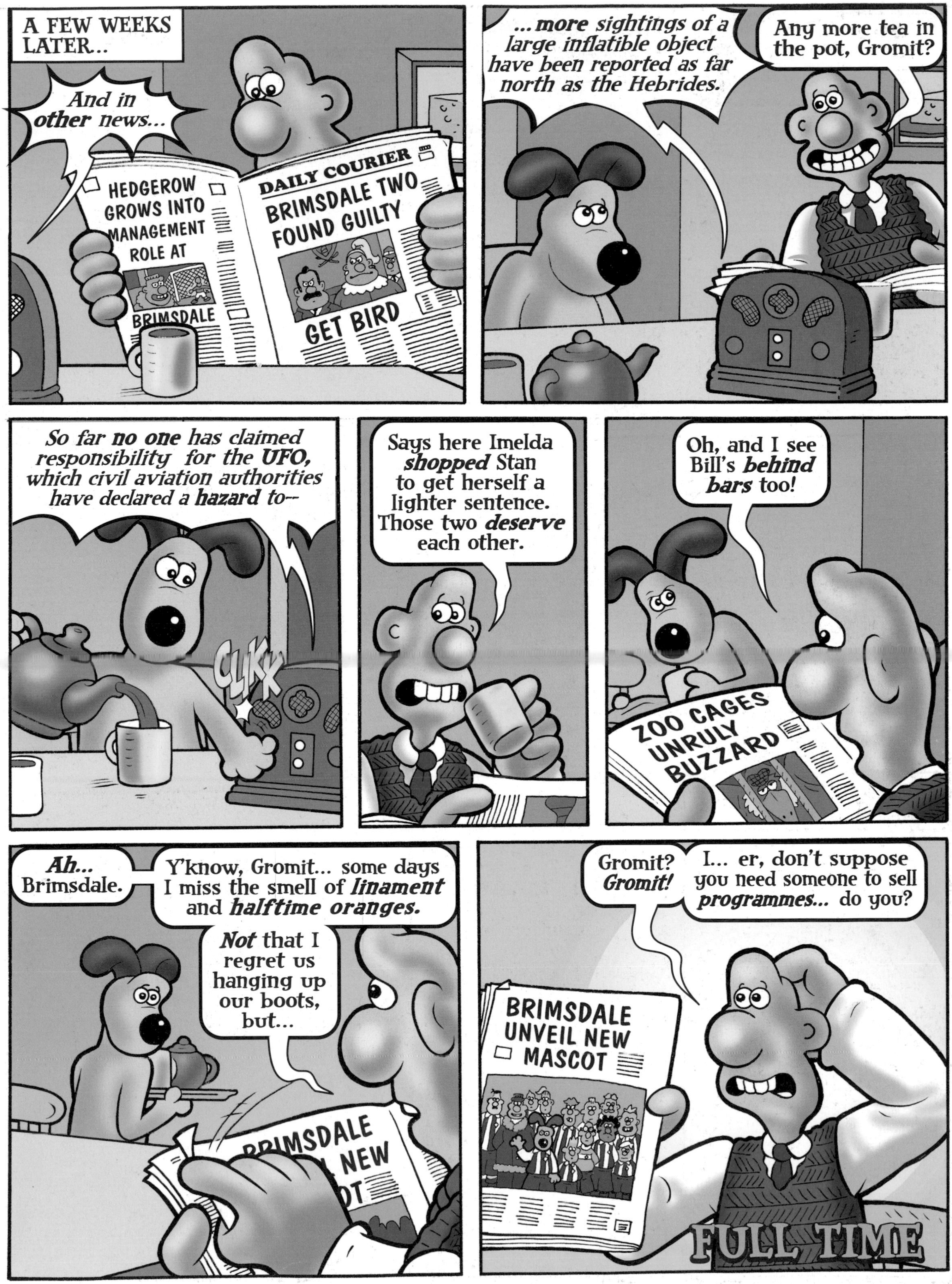
A FEW WEEKS LATER...
And in other news...
HEDGEROW GROWS INTO MANAGEMENT ROLE AT BRIMSDALE
DAILY COURIER
BRIMSDALE TWO FOUND GUILTY
GET BIRD
...more sightings of a large inflatible object have been reported as far north as the Hebrides.
Any more tea in the pot, Gromit?
So far no one has claimed responsibility for the UFO, which civil aviation authorities have declared a hazard to--
CLIKK
Says here Imelda shopped Stan to get herself a lighter sentence. Those two deserve each other.
Oh, and I see Bill's behind bars too!
ZOO CAGES UNRULY BUZZARD
Ah... Brimsdale.
Y'know, Gromit... some days I miss the smell of linament and halftime oranges.
Not that I regret us hanging up our boots, but...
Gromit? Gromit!
I... er, don't suppose you need someone to sell programmes... do you?
BRIMSDALE UNVEIL NEW MASCOT
FULL TIME

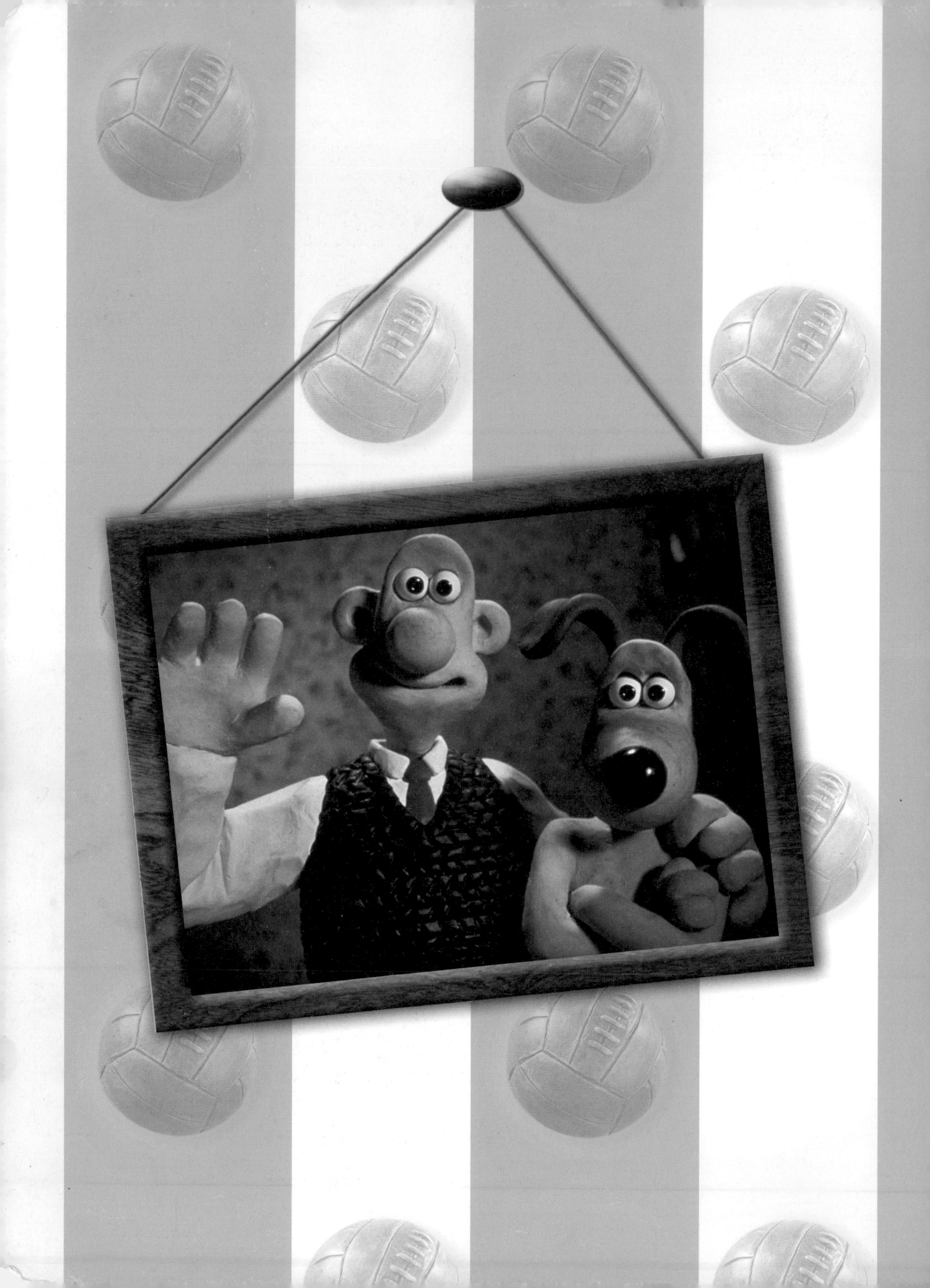